Dedicated to my rebel family, especially the Faith Bridge, XR Buddhists & XR Malvern. We are rising.

Sometimes our grief is proof of our sanity. It is no proof of sanity to be well adjusted to an insane society.
~ John Robbins

It is not half so important to know as to feel.
~ Rachel Carson

The times are urgent, let us slow down.
~ Bayo Akomolafe

Contents

Introduction

Gauzy swirls of steam are rising from the mug of hot tea beside me. Every so often the rich scent of sweetpeas curls into my nostrils – the tissue-thin blossoms sit on the windowsill next to my Buddha; purple, cream, and velvet-red. The tall window behind them is filled with a stand of colossal pines. When I duck to the left I see a fat pigeon perched on a bend in the uppermost branch, and behind her the wooded valley veers up towards the sky.

I began writing to the Earth a year ago, when I woke up to the reality of the climate and ecological emergency. I didn't know what else to do with the feelings that surged through me. These letters are brimming with grief, fury, fear, and heart-bursting gratitude and joy. They describe a new adventure into eco-activism. They acknowledge how it is to be an ordinary, flawed person living in a broken system. They are an invitation to relish the gifts of the world whilst we can – bouquets of glossy elderberries, the music of water, the goldcrest's bright crown.

Three days ago the Spalte Glacier in the Arctic disintegrated, the latest casualty of our rising global temperatures. I look online and the news is buried under Brexit chaos, US election speculation, and pandemic panic. As a second deadly wave of coronavirus looms, it is harder than ever for us to keep our concentration on the much bigger existential threat just over the horizon.

If we want to preserve human civilization, we need to find a way. It isn't easy to engage with the scale of the problem facing us. In my conversations with the Earth I swing between the uncomfortable delusion of being her sole savior, and the utter despair of being a flea on the back of a huge beast. I search for the middle way between burnout and inaction, and discover that the most precious things I have to offer are the ones I am most happy to give. You will find consolation here – we are all hypocrites, we are all failing in a multitude of ways, and – what we do does matter.

More than anything, these letters are a call to action. Maybe you worry that it's too late. Maybe it is. Maybe we are all living on a planetary hospice. Never mind. Do you want to stay inside watching forests burn on television, or do you want to go down singing love songs to the Earth?

Dear Earth, let me introduce myself

My name is Satya and I am one of the tiny creatures living on your back. I'm told there are 8.7 million different species of us here. I'm one of 7.8 billion humans. Hello.

I'm writing to you because I want to say three things: thank you, sorry, and please. I want to thank you for the sunflower I can see right now through my office window – a happy yellow splash. I want to say sorry that it's taken me so long to wake up to the damage we're all doing. I want to ask if you would please help me to look after you better.

I'm writing to you because I want to learn how to listen to you more carefully. I drown out your whispers with frenetic activity and machines and self-importance. I would like to lean in close again and run my fingers through your grass as the glossy blackbird serenades us.

I want us to talk late into the night, and I want you to tell me everything: the worst of it, and the best. I want to look, unflinching, at what we've all done, and use my sweet grief as fuel for the journey. I want to transmute regret into offerings and plant wildflowers. I want to grow communities. I want to shout unembarrassed from the rooftops about my love, so others too will fall in love with you all over again.

I am an ordinary, confused, deeply selfish being. My choices are often driven by fear, even as I convince myself otherwise.

I trust that you are big enough and wise enough to see these things about me, and to love me anyway. I trust that you will forgive us as a species, even as you are shrugging us off your back – if that's what it comes to.

Until then, I will be your servant – appreciating you, apologising, and asking for help. These letters will help me to remember. Right now I feel happy to be standing on your solid brown lap, as you whizz through the universe with clouds in your hair!

Love, Satya

Dear Earth, a confession

Whenever I do the washing up, I betray you.

I have a natural sponge, which would dissolve back into your body when I'm done with it. Instead I choose the bright plastic sponge, because I prefer the way it hugs the contours of the plates. I choose the sponge that will spoil your waters.

I am aware that there are bigger catastrophes. I read of a new factory that is hoping to pump out eighty trillion new nurdles every year. These fragments of plastic are the size of a lentil, near impossible to catch, and they live almost forever.

Still, I flush with guilt when I take the plastic sponge into my hand, because there is so much I am not in control of. Because I feel so inadequate when faced with the task ahead. Because it is easier to feel guilty than to feel helpless.

My friends also report their emotions pooling and stagnating around these dilemmas over small choices. One bought a new food processor and left it and its plastic packaging half-opened on her table for days, seized with regret. One feels grief at the years she brought plastic shower gel bottles into her home rather than soap.

Dear Earth, I know that contrition is an emotion you approve of, because it is a clean fuel – it burns fast, and leaves me with the energy to act. I also know that you don't want me to tie myself up in knots. Seeing my own limits and accepting them with kindness is crucial if I want to have fellow feeling for my companions. My tiny washing up sponge choice is a replica of that of the oil bosses – trying to keep their children safe in expensive schools, or feeding their compulsive hunger with more and more objects.

I can feel you smiling at me, darling Earth, as I wrestle with myself. It is a wry smile, and it is full of affection.

The warmth of it untangles my tangles and brings me to gratitude.

Love, Satya

Dear Earth, am I a good guy?

I really want to be a good guy.

I buy ethical toilet paper. I just signed the petition to stop the burning rainforest. I run a temple and I work as a psychotherapist and I try really hard to be good. Just look at me meditating in front of the Buddha!

I would at least like there to be bad guys. I can think of at least a few at the moment who are indisputably bad – throwing their weight around, causing horrific harm to your seas and land masses, shoring up their own egos. I'm not like them, am I?

On last night's Zoom meeting I listened to a woman activist who lives in an oppressive regime. She described how afraid people were to speak up against their government. I am so privileged – born white, to reasonably well-adjusted parents, in a very rich country.

This morning I considered shaving my head before I get arrested in the October rebellion, because I want to look more like a cool Buddhist in the photos. I live in a narrow world which I've worked hard to make safe for me, and much of my steadiness depends on props and circumstance. When my lunch is late and I am hungry, I get grumpy and snap at people. There are pockets of terror and shame in me, and the parts that protect them can be savage.

Parts of me have the characteristics of dictators. Parts of me have the characteristics of saints. I'd like to say that I'm always in control of when the different parts come out to play, but most of how-I-am is determined by my environment.

Sometimes I am the bad guy. Sometimes I am the good guy. When I remember this, sweet Earth, I soften. I can see the darkness in others without it overwhelming me. I can protect you from their violence without condemning them. I can lie under one of your splendid trees, watch the sun illuminate the leaves, and let this light into all of my dark places.

Love, Satya

Dear Earth, are holidays allowed?

I'm just back from a holiday. As we walked along Ellesmere lake eating ice-cream, dear Earth, I remembered that your lungs were burning.

How can I sit in cafés or visit castles or read trashy detective novels when I could be doing something to help you, Earth? Something, anything, that would subtract from the sum of pain in the world?

I am struggling to write about this. I want to say, we all have limits, and respecting them makes us better helpers. I want to say, when we offer compassion we should always include ourselves. I want to say, hey, everyone deserves a break once in a while.

These things are true. And – your lungs are still burning. Your skin is still clotting with carbon. Your lid of ice is still dissolving, drop by drop. How can I rest?

It is essential to rest, but not as much as I do. I didn't absolutely need a holiday. I could have carried on without one. Sometimes I rest because I am a foolish human being with many desires and preferences. I rest because I enjoy it.

I need your help, beloved Earth. I don't want to avoid my grief for the extinction of the blue macaw. I don't want to hide my disappointment in myself. Please help me to make room for these feelings, so I can carry them even whilst I disappear into television or take unnecessary afternoon naps. Please help me to make space for the sadness alongside the quiet pleasure of comforts, the appreciation of abundant gifts, the wild joy.

I want to tell you everything, Earth. If I can't be honest with you, then who?

Love, Satya

Dear Earth, he made me cry

We were watching men and women run alongside the lake. They were two thirds into their ten kilometres. You were too hot, Earth, as if you had a fever. People were struggling – pouring sweat, beetroot coloured, their bodies moving in tortured caricatures.

He was standing next to us. He was calling out encouragement as the runners pushed past. "Keep going, mate." If they had names on their shirts he used them. "Come on Sam. Good work Malcolm". As I listened, my throat thickened and I found myself on the verge of weeping.

The runners weren't strangers to him, but fellow beings, engaged in an important and difficult task. He cared about them. They were, for those moments, a part of his family.

Dear Earth, I know that we see each other like this when we are not preoccupied. Some of us are running, and some of us are supporting those who are running. Some of us are skipping this race, so we can let our injuries heal. We all have different parts to play.

We care about you too, when we step into the spaces surrounding the work of physical and psychological survival. We often find this full-empty place when we visit you – gazing at the enormity of the sea or examining a fine scarlet beetle.

Help us to find this spaciousness, so we can be kind to you and to each other. Help us remove the veils from our eyes so we can see that we are all brothers, sisters and others, travelling on the same opulent, luscious, awesome boat.

Love, Satya

Dear Earth, I want to enjoy you

I want to enjoy you while I still can.

That can be difficult when my head fills up with a tangle of plotting and self-recrimination and hopelessness and oughts.

I forget to gather flowers from the garden and make posies for my little vases. I forget to pluck a sweet blueberry or two on the way past the bush. I forget to bathe my tired eyes in the blue balm of your skies.

It would be a shame not to love you as you are today. Yes, there are hurricanes raging. Yes, your seas are rising. Yes, we need to get together and work hard to help you.

And right now, before my first appointment of the day, I have twenty minutes of grace. I can listen to the strimmer a few gardens away and trust that someone is taking care of something. I can taste my tea. I can notice the light falling on that turquoise length of sari draped across my bookshelf, and enjoy the gold threads glittering like strands of sun.

You remind me to delight in your beauty, Dear Earth, whenever I turn towards you. You remind me that this nourishment is what keeps me going.

Thank you, Earth, for your lapis lazuli and your jewelled streams. Thank you for your dark earth with earthworms threaded through. Thank you even for death, for the bright blood of prey and for the inevitability of decay, without which there would be no renewal.

Thank you, darling Earth. As I bow down to you, your soft rain kisses the back of my neck.

Love, Satya

Dear Earth, it's 4am and I'm frightened

The lights are on and I'm sitting up in bed with my laptop. There are three cats on the bed, one of them purring. The temple is quiet.

Earlier this evening twenty of us sat in a circle and explored the facts of your health, beloved Earth. We were asked how long we thought we had before things broke down. Twenty years? More? Less? One person said they had chickens and apple trees, and wondered how it would be to protect their family with a baseball bat.

I move in and out of denial. It can't be that bad, can it? I don't live in an apocalyptic film, but in a small wealthy town in a privileged country. It'll be other people whose countries slide underwater. Other people who push their children into flimsy boats as a desperate last resort. Surely science will save us. Surely our government will save us.

And then I feel the pain of the people who are already suffering, right now. My fellows on sinking islands and in countries without enough food. My animal friends. Plant-life withering and habitats degrading. You, sweet Earth.

Why am I writing to you, when I could be trying to sleep? Because *'solidarity is the tenderness of the people.' I am still touched by the compassion of the strangers in the circle, who held the space when I cried, and who cared. I feel tender towards you, dear Earth. I am writing because I have faith in this tenderness. I don't know if it will save us or not, but I know that I want to live in its warmth.

None of us know how long we have. What can we do in the face of this catastrophe? What can we do in the face of our deep ignorance, selfishness and violence? We can love each other, and we can love you, whilst we're here.

Thank you, Earth, for holding me as I type, in this small town in a small country, my animals sleeping around me. Thank you for the sweet moments of solidarity that light on me like moths. It's time to sleep, because tomorrow I have things to do.

Love, Satya

* quote by Che Guevara

Dear Earth, thanks for laps

Before my first cup of tea, I sat in the temple garden and looked out across the mist-pooled valley. The sun was bright and there was an autumnal freshness in the air. As often happens, our little dog Aiko climbed onto my lap and observed the morning with me.

Laps are good places to be. They are warm and soft. We can rest awhile in them, allowing our hard-working muscles and oughts to relax. We can begin to feel safe.

As I sat with my furry colleague, I chanted a mala of nembutsu. This is my spiritual practice, and it helps me to remember something important which I forget again and again. There is always a lap available to me if I need to crawl into it.

For me, it is the Buddha's lap. She has a lovely lap – huge and golden and squishy like eiderdown quilts. Others find different laps – the precious friend we lean into, support groups, books, silence. There was a time when I didn't believe in laps. I felt I should look after myself like a good grown-up. I'm glad I became desperate enough to let go of my own bootstraps and fall. That's when I had my first glimpse of something bigger than me – something that had been holding me up all along.

Dear Earth, your lap is something else. It is forested and mountained and scattered with sparkling lakes. It is the balding grass underneath the trees canopies I gaze up through. It is the home of crocodiles and canyons and pyramids and salamanders preserved in amber.

I am suddenly moved to tears as I write, as I realise that I can't get away from your lap. It is always underneath me. This battered second hand sofa, the cracked pavements of cities, the tenth store of claustrophobic office blocks. You never leave us. You are always underneath us, holding us up. You are all lap.

I sit for a while, fussing Aiko's ears. She looks up at me and smiles. How wonderful it is to provide laps for others, especially when they have silky-soft fur and extraordinary eyelashes. Remembering to take refuge in your lap, Mother Earth, helps me offer refuge to others. When we lean in, it makes you happy too.

Love, Satya

Dear Earth, it's too much

On waking, I read of Hurricane Dorian. He is crushing people like ants under an elephant's foot. These extreme weather furies have always been with us, dear Earth. The scientists tell us that we have already made the weather gods more capricious, and that in the coming years more and more of us will be trampled or displaced or starved.

I look at the photo of the man who has lost his son. I look into his eyes. His suffering enters me, and bleeds into the suffering of the burning trees, the desperate farmers, the last few Amur leopards, the desiccating coral reef.

Sometimes it is too much.

There is an old story about Avalokiteshvara, the Bodhisattva of Compassion, who hears the cries of suffering beings. She made a vow to save them all, and was furnished with many arms so she could reach out and offer them whatever they need. She helped without ceasing, saving multitudes, until one day she glanced down at the gates of hell and saw that even as she worked, countless millions were streaming into their depths. It was too much for her, and in that moment she shattered.

As she shattered, she cried out for help. She cried to Amida, the Buddha of Infinite Light, and he came to her broken body and tenderly put it back together again. From that time on Amida had her back, and she continued in her great compassionate work, no longer alone.

As an ordinary foolish being, I have many limits. I only have the energy for a certain amount of action. I need to say no often, and make space to retreat, and stroke cats and eat pizza and read murder mysteries.

I can also only hold so much suffering in my heart. I want to keep my eyes and ears open to the truth, and I want to let it move me. My grief and rage fuels me, and it connects me to my comrades. I also need to remember that, however many arms I have, there is too much suffering for me to bear. When I am approaching my limit, I can call out for help before I shatter. I know that you'll hold me together, darling Earth.

Love, Satya

Dear Earth, thank you for denial

When I think about the vanishing rainforests right now, I don't feel a thing. Swathes of denial are shifting around me, like layered suits of armour.

This denial gets a bad name. We think that we'd be better off without it, and others too. Surely if everyone had their denial ripped away from them, people would start waking up to this emergency and do something?

In my early days of becoming vegan, I shouted from the rooftops. I shoved gory photos under people's noses and mentioned the ground-up male chicks at every opportunity. I gradually learnt that these things just didn't work. They didn't work because, when you push at denial, it digs its feet in like an obstinate mule.

I love Aesop's fable about the Sun and the North Wind, who both boasted that they were more powerful than the other. As they were quarrelling a traveller walked past, wearing a cloak. The Sun suggested that whoever was stronger would be able to strip him of his cloak. The North Wind blew – fiercely ripping at the cloak. As the wind whipped around him, the traveller pulled his cloak more and more firmly around him. The blustery North Wind tired himself out and admitted defeat.

Then it was the Sun's turn. He gently shone, warming the traveller as he walked. The traveller rested by the side of the road and peeled off his cloak.

Those of us who've woken up to the calamity of your suffering, dear Earth, can be tempted to yank at other people's denial. We might try to shame them or blame them, or use shock tactics. We might look at climate deniers with disdain or even disgust.

Our denial is always present for a good reason – to protect our system from collapse. Just like the other parts of us that get a bad name (and that cause chaos for us and for others) – addictions, greed, even violence – they all have positive intentions for us. These parts are trying to keep us from being flooded with shame, fear, fury or grief – so much intense feeling that our system fears we wouldn't survive it.

I do think that there's a place for shock tactics, or for letting others see the depth of my emotion. We can knock loudly on the walls of denial and see what happens. I also think that I need to be careful when I become the North Wind, blowing harder and harder as my victim presses their hands even more firmly over their ears. Their denial is keeping them safe, and it's not my place to rip it away from them. And of course, we are more like them than we'd care to admit. We are all in denial about something.

What I can do is listen to them – listen and then listen some more. I can empathise with their need for denial, or whatever else is protecting them. I can remember how it was for me before I 'woke up'. I can remember that not everyone will be able to hear the truth just yet, and that's okay.

I hold so much privilege. I have lots of therapy behind me, no major addictions, and no crippling depression or anxiety. I'm not preoccupied by how I'm going to feed my children or whether I'm going to leave my marriage. I live in a wealthy country and I am well supported by my community and my faith.

My privilege comes with responsibility, to do the things that are impossible for others to do. I'll keep walking forwards, one step at a time, being as kind as I can to everyone I meet. Some of my fellow travellers need their cloaks right now. That's okay. It's no business of mine, and the sun will keep on shining.

Love, Satya

Dear Earth, I feel superior

Yesterday I dressed in black and had my face painted into a skull. With fellow skull people, we walked slowly and silently through the streets of Worcester. We were delivering a letter about our disappointment in the County Council, who have failed to declare a climate emergency.

As I walked, I felt sad. Everyone was going about their business as if nothing was happening. They weren't thinking about you, beloved Earth, as they filled plastic bags with new clothes. They bought mobile phones because their old ones (containing precious metals, extracted from your body at great cost) were already out of fashion. They consumed and consumed, and belched out waste.

It is so easy to feel superior, especially whilst dressed as a skull person.

When I begin to feel superior, I remind myself of my privilege – my support system, my education, my faith, my financial security – all the things that have allowed me the luxury of connecting with my grief about your wounds, dear Earth.

When I begin to feel superior, I remind myself of the 'could do better' sections on my own scorecard – the unnecessary car journeys, the money I spend on fripperies, the carbon footprint of our seven pets, three of which eat meat. I remind myself that feeling superior is ironic proof of my human frailties.

When I remember these things, I can suddenly see that the people thronging the shop-lined streets are my comrades. They may be on the same eco-journey I'm on –

they may have been on it for decades longer than me. They may need more information and more support before their denial cracks, as I did. They may be forever locked into extreme self-protection – and that's okay. We will never change everybody's minds and we don't have to. We just need enough of us to speak up with clear voices, dear Earth. We just need enough of us to feel the sadness I feel.

Twelve of us were seen by hundreds, yesterday. They paused and watched us pass. They whispered to each other – 'climate', 'Extinction Rebellion'. They threw us looks of pity or disgust, or beeped their car horns in support.

Some of them promised to join us, and some of them will.

Love, Satya

Dear Earth, help me receive your love

We were visited by an eighty eight year old Reverend Canon, the friend of a member of our Buddhist congregation. She joined us for service, chanting nembutsu, circumambulating around the tall golden Buddha, and bowing as far as her body would allow her to.

Afterwards over decaffeinated coffee she spoke of a retreat she'd recently attended. She said that, in the silence, she'd realised how hard it was for her to receive Christ's love. During the retreat, she prayed that she might allow it in.

I find it hard to receive your love, beloved Earth.

I fill my schedule with activity, distracting myself from what's hard to swallow. I worship other fickle gods – popularity, sense pleasures, security. I get caught in the treacle of feeling-unworthy. I fall back into the belief – how tempting it is! – that I can control everything if I try hard enough.

All these things get between me and you, Earth. They stop me from noticing blackberries fattening on the hedgerows. They don't let me linger when the warm sun kisses my cheeks. They pull my attention from our old cat, whose bones are protruding, and who just wants his head gently fondled.

I will pray for the ability to receive your love, great Earth. The more nourishment I allow in, the better I'll be able to hold the darkness as well as the light. The more sweetness I allow in, the more devoted I'll be to loving you back.

My cheeks are warm, Earth, and my old cat is purring.

Love, Satya

Dear Earth, not being in denial sucks

I knew about climate change for half my life. I'd heard about the greenhouse effect and the dwindling rainforest. I knew we were heading in a bad direction. I made no concessions to these facts.

What changed? Why am I now waking in the night, my adrenaline fizzing? Why am I obsessively reading the news? Why am I putting swathes of my free time into organising a rebellion? Why am I on this roller-coaster of fierce grief and hot anger and swamped overwhelm?

It is so easy to slip back into the soft enveloping dressing-gown of denial. Extreme weather has been around forever, hasn't it? Humans have always suffered in vast numbers, haven't they? You are feisty and resilient, dear Earth, and you will sort things out for us, won't you? The governments know what's happening and they won't lead us into catastrophe, will they?

I want to preserve my comfortable existence. When I look into the gaping jaws of climate science, I see how precarious my security is. I see that we will be chewed up and spat out unless we make drastic changes to our lifestyles, soon. I see that most of us won't make these changes willingly, and so it will have to be agreed by representatives of all our nations and then mandated. I see what lengths governments will go to, in order to avoid the unpopularity of speaking these truths.

I don't want to be an eco-activist. I want to be a psychotherapist who writes books and runs a Buddhist temple. I want to spend my free time walking on the common with my little dog, or reading poetry, or baking brownies.

And, I see that it is time for me to act. It is time for us to take matters into our own hands, before it is too late. Some say that the tipping points are already behind us, and maybe they are right. Whatever happens next, I still want to do what I can.

Not being in denial sucks. And, being in denial sucks more. There is a sweet relief that comes with meeting the truth, and surges of energy, and great reserves of compassion for ourselves and for each other. And for you, dear Earth, with your volcanoes and your underwater palaces, your manta rays, woodlice and long-tailed tits.

In stepping out of denial, we step into relationship with you. We dance with you and all your shining beauty.

Love, Satya

Dear Earth, we are all hungry babies

At the weekend my jagged edges rubbed up against the rough edges of someone I love, and sparks flew. After long circling fights, we were both wrung out and dispirited.

When we are tired, hungry, lonely or flooded with emotion, we can lose access to our compassion. We don't notice the fear behind other people's meanness. We feel impatient as they struggle to find their quiet whispering voice. When we are both in this state we become like two starving babies, each expecting the other to feed him.

As you get hotter, Earth, we will speak from our hungry babies more and more. We will try to protect ourselves by blaming, shaming, isolating or hitting out. We will lose our precious community connections as we paddle furiously, trying to keep our own head above water.

We need to work out how to keep ourselves nourished, so we can find our way back to ourselves, and to each other. Our overwhelmed baby parts may be nourished by lying in the Buddha's lap, or walking on the moors, or eating roast potatoes. After a good Sunday nut roast and an evening in front of the television under a furry blanket, I felt tender towards my loved one again, and they felt tender towards me.

One thing that nourishes me is writing these letters to you, beloved Earth. It connects me to your green skirts with golden threads. It stitches me into my community. It helps me attend to my own starving babies, offering them soft caresses and understanding.

It helps me to serve you in this small way, exquisite, awesome Earth.

Love, Satya

Dear Earth, breakfast was astonishing

Just ordinary porridge with cinnamon and toasted sunflower seeds.

Where did you grow my oats, Earth? You grew them in Cherrywood, New Zealand. They ate and drank with their toes from your dark soil, and your brother fed them with light.

Sunflower seeds, cute nuggets of goodness my little dog loves – born on flowers that dare you not to grin.

Cinnamon! The treasure of cassia trees, hiding under the outer bark, peeled off and curling into quills. How did we discover your larder of spices, beloved Earth? Is there more to find?

The stainless steel of my spoon was melted and mixed and poured in Vietnam. Which person did that? Where are they now?

Thank you Earth for ordinary things. The things we sleep on, think with, snuggle under, lick, light and read. The things we gaze at until our whole beings are anointed with balm.

Thank you, gorgeous Earth, for porridge.

Love, Satya

Dear Earth, I trusted them

I trusted the scientists. When they discovered our house was burning, I thought they would scream 'Fire! fire!' until we were all out and safe.

I trusted the media. I thought they would make the climate crisis front page news until we acted to save our children. I thought they would tell the truth.

I trusted the governments. It's their job to look after us. If they knew we were killing ourselves, I thought they would take away our razor blades.

Some people have been screaming. A doctor went on a hunger strike. Did you hear about him? One hundred and sixteen environmental activists were assassinated in 2014. People have been screaming for decades.

And most of us have been like me – cosseted in my thick fleece of forgetfulness. I forgive myself. Without that protection I feel hopeless, deeply sad, frustrated, frightened and overwhelmed. Of course I looked away. Of course I left it to others.

Without my fleece I realise that I can't rely on them to save us. I am them. I have eyes and a brain, and I can read the reports from the IPCC and make up my own mind. I can write these love letters to you, dear Earth, and ask people to share them. I can sit on the road and risk imprisonment. I can grieve, and not hide my tears.

Will it be enough? Will it be enough, beloved Earth, or is it too late for our civilisation? Am I contributing to the denial if I write a happy ending to this letter to you? Would I be joining those I cannot trust?

We are late. I don't know whether we can survive. And here I am, writing to you as dawn breaks over the valley. The red streaks on the horizon gently fade into violet, tangerine, baby blue. There are birds singing. Later I will eat and walk and pray and laugh.

How can I know what I know, and keep on living?

You are burning, dear Earth. I must.

Love, Satya

Dear Earth, I have a question

I committed to not buying any new clothes for a year. I'm taking part in the rebellion in October, and I'm afraid of being cold on the streets at night. My coat is thin. I can't find a good second hand one. Do I buy a shiny new one?

Do I carry on visiting the good vet who wants immigrants out? As a vegan, do I strike matches made with animal products (every single one) or use plastic lighters? Do I poison the rats living under the temple kitchen with their families?

How do I balance my self-care with your needs, Earth? When I'm weary, can I use the car? Do I buy pizza wrapped in plastic? Do I go to the march or lie beached on the sofa?

We all have these impossible questions, lovely Earth. Some of them square up to us and stare as if they want a fight. Some of them flicker away in the background like embers in a breeze. Most we shut our eyes to.

We can't win. This is where we begin. It's a great relief to admit it. Everything we do causes some good, and some harm. Whenever we act, we are motivated by a mixture of love and fear.

We can't win, but we can buy the new coat, or not, and see how fallible we are, and forgive ourselves and others. We can't win, beloved Earth, but we can swoosh these questions around in our hearts before we pay the pest controller. We can't win, but we can edge towards love, like following a distant star.

Look how bright it is!

Love, Satya

Dear Earth, I am tiny

I am one of your seven point eight billion humans. Just one, out of 7800000000.

Since I was born, you have given me all I need. Your dark crumbly earth has fed me. Your clear water has quenched my thirst. Your raw materials have clothed me, housed me, entertained me and inspired me. Your rich atmosphere gave me my first breath, and this one. You will be with me until my very last.

I owe you everything, and I am utterly dependent on your health for my own continuance.

Knowledge of this deep dependency is frightening. It shows me how little control I have. It demands humility. It holds me accountable to my actions, both conscious and unconscious. If I have harmed you (I have, I have) then it shows me what I need to do.

I need to feel grief, and to use this grief as fire to fuel me. I need to do one thing that will help you to heal, and then another. I need to take care of myself, so I can do this for as long as possible. I need to be realistic about what 1 in 7.8 billion can do. And, I need to let you support me, darling Earth, because with your help we can change everything.

Love, Satya

Dear Earth, it's impossible to save you

Today I will be flying to Barcelona. I bought the ticket before I woke up to the climate and ecological emergency. I am going to honour my commitment to the meeting I'm attending, and also, flying feels like having to eat a bloody steak bought before becoming vegan.

After this flight, I vow to never fly again.

Will I really never get into an aeroplane again? I don't know. I can't imagine what the future will bring. Maybe someone I love will need me to fly. Maybe they'll invent a carbon-neutral plane. Maybe I'll be asked to speak at a super-swanky conference for lots of money and my resolve will crack.

We make vows because we are inspired by love. Sometimes these vows are impossible. In our Buddhist tradition we chant: "Innumerable are sentient beings, we vow to save them all". It's clearly ridiculous. How can I save even a tiny fraction of the wondrous beings you support, dear Earth?

There's a story of a little girl who is throwing beached, dying starfish back into the sea, one by one as they lie around her in their thousands. She has made this vow. That's why she's there, engaged in that impossible task. When a grown up gently mocks her, telling her that she isn't making a difference, she tells us, 'It makes a difference to this one. And this one.' The drying starfish sail through the air and slide into the sweet water.

Precious Earth, your health is failing. Your creatures are dying in unprecedented numbers. I am full of love for you, and I am inspired to make some vows. I vow not to fly again. I vow to tell the truth about you. I vow to offer my service to the group I think has the best chance of saving you.

Love is a powerful fuel – a million times more concentrated than hate. Hate makes a big impressive show but then quickly sputters out. It leaves barriers in other people's hearts. Seeing love in action opens them up.

Darling Earth, many of us are making vows for you. We won't always keep them perfectly or manage to follow them through, and that's okay. It will make a difference to this piece of your awesome aliveness. And this one.

Love, Satya

Dear Earth, we need each other

I am looking at a photo of me and my Buddhist teacher, Dharmavidya. We were together at a friend's temple in Spain, meeting with Buddhists from all around Europe. He has his arm around me and we are both smiling in the bright sun.

You are particularly beautiful in Sant Iscle de Vallalta, dear Earth. The lapis lazuli sky kisses the mountains. Wandering around the temple are horses and semi-wild black pigs. There is a magnificent fig tree. The gompa is surrounded by glass, and your trees held us as we prayed.

Early one morning, I went alone to the library and my teacher appeared as if by magic. He listened as I told him about losing my temper the night before. He told me stories of meetings with his own teachers that are as fresh as the moment they happened, decades later. We laughed a lot, as we always do. All good teachers have a twinkle in their eyes that frequently flowers into chuckling.

I came away feeling seen and nourished and loved. All humans need this nourishment. It comes from everywhere. The old school friend who offered to come and visit me when I'm rebelling in London next week, and bring me a flask of soup. The little girl on the plane who giggled all the way home. My cat Roshi who just entered the room, bowed, and is asking me to scratch his head.

Dear Earth, if we are to be strong enough, courageous enough, to do what we need to do for you, then we must reach out to each other. We must point out the trees in the Waitrose carpark to our husband, and then pause to take in their leaves flushing scarlet. We must write to the author to express our warm gratitude. We must practice receiving (so hard!) as a necessity, and as a gift to the giver.

Humans need each other, darling Earth, especially when we lose our tempers. When we laugh together, we are pouring blessings onto your body.

Love, Satya

Dear Earth, I'm a happy bunny

Yesterday I was overwhelmed. There was too much to do before the rebellion this Monday. I was frightened about what I was letting myself in for. After waking up to your grave prognosis, dear Earth, I was missing my old comfy-in-denial life.

Today I am happy. What changed?

A good night's sleep. A reassuring message from a loved one. A meeting with other rebels where I heard their grief and felt less alone. A grocery shop of posh food from Waitrose. An excited greeting from a happy little dog.

My internal weather changes, and it will continue to change – especially at times like this. That's okay. Your weather changes too, beloved Earth, and much of it is necessary for your health. Without the long days of rain, you wouldn't bloom in such glorious technicolour. Strong winds sweep away your rubbish. The warm sun keeps the ice at bay.

My grief has fuelled my journey into activism. My anger shows me where my boundaries are. Even my low, grey days force me to lay low, allowing me to recuperate.

I'm not saying that all my weather is necessary or useful. Sometimes there's just a violent storm, and it causes damage, and it sucks. And, I do find it helpful to keep my mind open – to see if I can find any treasure amongst the wreckage. Yesterday reminded me that I am human, and that I need to go easy on myself. It reminded me that I have community around me, and that I can ask them for help. I am grateful for that.

Tomorrow I might be visited by a cyclone. Today I will enjoy being a happy bunny – bounce bounce bounce – and hope that my happiness might be a little infectious.

Love, Satya

Dear Earth, this sustains me

The underwater sucker sounds of my cat Tsuki diligently washing her elbows.

The wild streaks of red in the morning sky, sighing into blue.

The knobbly glass candle on my shrine and its halo of God.

The mug of redbush tea that my husband brings me, steaming and fragrant, a precious golden cargo.

The wonders of toast!

Drinking the fresh scent of my little dog's soft belly.

Walking out into the dewy garden, sprinkles of birdsong, a wild rabbit, the kindly trees, things flourishing and dying back, always flourishing and dying back.

You sustain me, darling Earth. You keep me alive.

I will do what I can to keep you alive, with joy, with an aching heart, with courage, with gratitude.

Love, Satya

Dear Earth, I am frightened

I didn't think I'd be planning for my arrest.

I didn't think I'd be using this week of holiday to stand on a cold, rainy bridge in London and speak up for you.

I didn't think I'd learn new words like kettling or bust cards, and discuss the relative merits of superglue or steel cable ties for affixing myself to your surface.

I am an ordinary, law abiding person. I trusted the governments to do what was best for us all, or at least to not watch from the sidelines as we slide into a horror movie.

I didn't think I'd meet so many others who have the fire of love for you in their bellies, dear Earth. Ordinary people like me who have rearranged their lives to put you first.

I am going to upset people when we get to London and sit in the roads, dear Earth – other ordinary people who just want to get to their interview or to their doctor's appointment or home to their loved ones. I am going to cause inconvenience and frustration and sometimes fury.

Anso Coetzer said, "Decisions become easier when your will to please God outweighs your will to please the world."

My will to please you, darling Earth, now outweighs my will to please anyone else. This is how it should be. I am frightened, and I have enough courage and enough friends to carry me forwards.

I hope we make a difference, beloved Earth. We'll try our best.

Love, Satya

Dear Earth, I sobbed as they arrested me

I wasn't upset about getting a criminal record, the blank hours ahead of me in a cell, standing in court, the fine.

I didn't feel unsafe. As the police carried me away, they checked four times if they were hurting me, if I was okay.

I wasn't ashamed, after a lifetime of being a good girl, of not inconveniencing anyone, of doing as I'm told.

I sobbed, beloved Earth, because the grief I felt for you suddenly rose up and crushed me.

I knew that six hundred of us had already been through these cells, and we were hardly appearing on our national television.

I saw the whisper of my voice up against the airplane roar of those who have unimaginable power.

I recognised the system's denial about the gravity of your prognosis, as I have also lived under a thick protective crust of it for decades.

The grief pushed its way through me, and it left me clean.

I am lucky to be here, dear Earth, as I write with the red biro a smiling officer brought me.

Later they'll bring me food, and I'll go home to my extravagant privilege.

Others are failing to coax crops from impoverished soil. Others have had their homes violently flattened. Others are watching the ice caps melt, drip by deathly drip, and they don't know what to do.

I know what to do.

I vow to witness your vast suffering, darling Earth, and pray for your coast dwellers, your intricate coral reefs and your nightingales.

I vow to meet the razor-sharp violence of others with peace in my heart.

I vow to do what you call me to do.

I am so inadequate, dear Earth, and I contain the same greed, hate and delusion that is strangling you.

I am asking for your forgiveness, with my sobs, and with this red pen.

Love, Satya

Dear Earth, help hold me steady

Dear Earth, help hold me steady.

The ground underneath me is moving like shook silk.

My life here looks the same as before – plentiful food, clothes to wash, money to earn, ordinary beauty.

And yet, the sound of police helicopters are tattooed into my ears. I dream of the dread of losing territory, and of keeping secrets. I wait for news of the next of my friends to be arrested.

I know (I can't unknow, I can't unknow) that you are in peril, dear Earth, that we are heading for an iceberg, and that we don't have long to turn the huge ship round. Most of your passengers are too busy soothing themselves to notice.

I don't know whether my desperate actions are improving your prognosis, darling Earth, or just alienating people. I don't know whether it's already too late.

Help hold me steady. Help me delight in the generous crop of dandelion leaves in the vegetable patch – our bunnies' favourite food. Remind me how small I am in your vastness, and that your fate doesn't rest on my shoulders alone. Help me relish the dazzling sugars in your dying leaves. Show me the golden connections with my fellow humans that hold me like a web of elastic wherever I turn. Help me transmute my grief to praise.

I lie on my back on my office carpet, you underneath me, and I breathe.

Right now you are holding me steady. From here I can go forwards. I can do the next right thing, which is boiling water for tea.

Love, Satya

Dear Earth, I kiss your skin

I kiss the velvet forehead of my cat as I stoop to his purring gratitude.

I kiss the rim of my speckled stoneware mug, full of rich coffee.

I kiss the face of my phone which connects me to so many.

I kiss the soft intimacy of my husband's neck.

I blow kisses to mountain tops, huge manta ray, brave activists, frilled peonies, industrial waste, the woman jumping in front of a train, jazz music, hairy-legged spiders, bank managers, a baby's little toe, this drop of rain, this one, this one.

I kiss the tarmac of Lambeth bridge and touch my forehead down, once, twice, three times, a prayer my Muslim brother showed me.

I kiss your skin, dear Earth. I kiss you all over.

Love and gratitude, Satya

Dear Earth, we're divided

This morning I wanted to write something that would bring us all together, dear Earth, in our shared desire to heal you. And then I realised that it was impossible.

There are already many people who think that the way we're doing things is very wrong. There are people from within our movement who disagree gravely with each other. There are those who don't think you're sick, darling Earth. Most of them won't change their minds.

How can we help you, Earth, if we are so divided?

I pause and let this sink in. I see the depth of my own divided nature – how quick I am to judge others, and how often I judge myself. I feel depression, frustration, and – here it is – hopelessness.

For me, hopelessness is not the end but the beginning. When I deeply sink into my hopelessness, then a dot of light appears in the darkness. This bright spot doesn't come from me. It comes from something bigger, dear Earth – from you, from the Buddha, from humankind... As I lean into the darkness, the dot begins to grow, and soon I can see how it illuminates everything.

It doesn't change what it lights up. I am still a foolish divided being, and my fellow humans are still laden with their own greed, hate and delusion. It does mean that I feel accepted, with all my faults. As this acceptance soaks in, like freezing cold toes in a hot bath, I can begin to radiate this acceptance out to others.

I've made mistakes. Some huge ones. I've caused damage. I'll do it again. Both individually, and as a part of the groups I belong to. Now that I'm illuminated, that doesn't seem like the end of the world any more. I can even feel fond towards some of the messy chaos, and offer it a wry smile.

And then to my surprise I'm back to the beginning of my letter. Here is something we *do* all have in common. Our frailty. Our colourful messiness. Our aching vulnerability. Our dependence on you, marvellous Earth, and on each other. What creatures we are. Aren't we beautiful?

With so much love, Satya

Dear Earth, what should I do now?

This rebellion is over. What should I do now?

I have struggled with this question for most of my life. I have a tendency to take on too much – cramming in more and more appointments and responsibilities. I gasp for air, and yet when blank spaces do loom I feel panicky and fill them up.

I've been worrying about my role in Extinction Rebellion going forwards – this work that feels so vital for your survival, sweet Earth. How can I ever do enough? Should I take on more leadership, cut down on my other work, force myself into places that don't quite feel right for your sake?

I look at the photo of myself during our march through Oxford Street. I was with the Buddhists, carrying our glorious banner, and halfway through we were caught up by some guys with a massive sound system pumping out reggae. It was clear to me what I needed to do in that particular moment – dance.

When I listen to you, dear Earth, I know what to do next. It's usually very mundane. Change the flowers on the shrine. Put hay out for the bunnies. Make my friend a cup of tea. My role in this great drama isn't always the one I'd choose for myself. Sometimes I'm cleaning the toilet whilst someone else is getting all the applause on centre stage. Feelings of jealousy, frustration and greed arise, and that's okay – I can live with them. The most important thing is that the show goes on. We all have different parts to play, and the toilet needs cleaning.

I am sitting on the sofa by the glass doors, soaking up late October sun. Little dog is sat next to me, her white chin stained pink by her breakfast of beetroot. I'm baking some cubes of sweet potato in the oven for her – her favourite treat – and the honeyed scent is filling the flat.

A friend wrote that maybe I needed to plant myself in the dark after the activity of the past few weeks, in order to get ready for growing again. Today I am hiding in the dark. This is what I need to do next – this is what I hear when I listen to you, wise Earth. You always know.

Love, Satya

Dear Earth, this is the grief

This is the grief I found like an underwater lake, vast and luminous.

This is the grief that wakes me at four a.m. to stare at the ceiling, my heart trembling.

This is the grief that follows me, with its dark shadow of guilt. It has a bright lining of anger, and every so often it tips me into grey hopelessness.

This is the grief I want to protect my friends from feeling, dear Earth. It is too much.

And. This grief is a gift.

This is the grief that propelled me onto the wrong side of the law, for your sake.

This is the grief that charges me as I write these words. It has given me new dear friends. It has swept the clag from my veins so my blood runs freely and happily. It has reminded me how awesome you are, Earth, and how each day is unearnt, empty, full of luscious colour and promises.

Every drop of this precious stuff, darling Earth, can be used to heal you.

Every drop will give me courage. Every drop will show me what to do next. Every drop can be used to connect me back in to your iridescent beetles, your chuckling streams, your delicate green fingers poking up through concrete.

I want everyone to feel this grief, darling Earth. It will save us all.

Love, Satya

Dear Earth, I am greedy

When I was a girl my mum would make pancakes as a special treat. One for me, one for my little brother. One for me, one for my little brother.

I hated the time it took for the pale creamy batter to take on golden patterns, be flipped, and appear on my plate with sharp lemon juice, an occasional pip, and crunchy granulated sugar.

I hated even more that every other pancake wasn't for me! I wanted *all* the pancakes.

I still carry this bottomless pancake greed. This morning I made myself thick fluffy pancakes – served with ripe banana slices and swimming in good maple syrup. As I ate them a part of me chanted 'all mine! all mine!' with deep satisfaction.

It is hard for most of us to share our treasure. I happily give away books or veg from the garden, but don't ask me for my last expensive truffle. I'm generous with my time until I'm full up with people, and then I'd begrudge you five minutes. How much I give to charity varies wildly, depending not on my bank account but on how financially secure I'm feeling.

I try to be honest with myself about my greed.

It helps me to be gentle on myself – greed is always an attempt at compensating for a physical or emotional lack, usually in our distant past, or to bring security to parts of us that are wobbling.

It helps me to be realistic about what I can manage (offering half an hour to listen) and what I can't (being available all afternoon).

It helps me to play with the practice of renunciation, and to discover the sweet fruits of surrender.

My greed is precious because it reminds me how it is to be human. Other human beings will sometimes be greedy too. As I try to help you, dear Earth, I sometimes slide into oily smugness. 'I'm a non-flying plastic-avoiding vegan, aren't I? I got arrested for the Earth's sake, didn't I? What are *you* doing?'

When I catch myself judging others, I return to taking the log out of my own eye before offering to take the splinter out of yours. I've got several lifetimes worth of pancake greed to deal with for starters. I admit that this morning I overdid it a teensy bit...

Darling Earth, thank you for maple syrup pancakes. And, in retrospect, thank you for other people to share them with. Maybe next time I'll see if my little brother is free.

Love, Satya

Dear Earth, we are born wounded

Maybe our grandfather was shamed when his pudgy two year old arms reached out for comfort, and so he learnt to spit hate at his own neediness. Maybe our great grandmother was shut in the cupboard for hours at a time, and monsters grew in the dark. Further back there is the horror of war, oppression breeding oppression, silent sexual abuse, and so many beautiful dead children.

We carry these wounds, beautiful Earth, passed down from our ancestors. Our parents lightened our load in some regards, forgiving and healing, and they also gifted us new pain of their own invention. They did the best they could with what they received – would we have done any better?

Our legacy is to tend to these multi-generational injuries, kind Earth. If we tend to them, we will hand on smaller burdens to our own children. We can treat each wound as a pitiful unloved creature, starved of light, and slowly approach it with balm and with listening ears. We can find wise and steady companions to walk with us through the internal neighbourhoods where stabbings happen. We remember how long it took for some of these wounds to be created, and we are patient. We hear how long these injured parts of us have been waiting for us to help them, and we weep for them.

I think you understand this about us, dear Earth. I think you see how utterly smashable we are, figurines of paper-thin china. You see how we mobilise ignorance, fierce criticism and blame to hold us together. I think you see how frail our bodies are, like the intricate gills underneath mushrooms, and how afraid we are of impermanence. I think you see how we often stagger under the weight of our burdens, and how we grab onto whatever we can as we fall.

We are amazing, dear Earth. Carrying this heavy heritage of savagery and bitterness, we are almost always more than this. We find a thousand ways to arrange our burdens so we can pause to help a mother and baby onto the train. We take two weeks of holiday so we can plant moss. We write and tell our sister that we love her, even though she hasn't spoken to us for a year. People are starving themselves for you right now, dear Earth. They are going to prison. They are risking their lives to protect you.

We are born hobbled, carrying knots of darkness. And, light streams around these knots, working away at them, loving them untied. We are doing our best for you, beloved Earth, with what we were handed down. We are doing okay.

Much love, Satya

Dear Earth, how can we possibly enjoy you?

Much of you is poisoned, dear Earth. Your forests are thinning like hair. Many of your glorious species are fading into history. Your cloak of weather is whipping more and more crazily around you.

When we take the science into our hearts and see what we have done, when we begin to grieve, how can we carry on with our ordinary lives? How can we tend our garden, knowing about desertification? How can we enjoy your brilliant sunsets knowing how much carbon is trapped up there, suffocating you?

We must be like those in recovery from helpless dependency on harsh chemicals. We mustn't shy away from the damage done – to our bodies, to our loved ones, to our world. We must make amends wherever we can, making use of our uniqueness. We must pass on what we know to others, those who are still trapped in dark denial.

Alongside all this, we have a duty to enjoy the sober years we have been gifted. We must gently stretch the capacity of our hearts to contain more grief and more joy than ever before. We must delight in each juicy slice of pineapple, say hello to every fat rosy robin, and bow to the raging sea. We must teach our children how to enjoy mud squishing through their bare toes. We must allow the world to tickle us, and laugh.

You want us to play, darling Earth. Why else would you offer us chestnuts and piles of dry leaves? There will be dying, and when there isn't, here is my little dog – flicking her toy elephant around the office, hardly able to contain her happiness as it arcs through the air.

Much love, dear Earth, Satya

Dear Earth, here's the secret to everything

Sometimes I don't know what the hell I'm doing.

Sometimes I despair at the size of your wound and the insufficiency of the bandages and balm, dear Earth. I see myself as a speck of dust in an ocean.

Sometimes I want to shove other people off your lap and into oxygen-less space, dear Earth, when hateful, ignorant, or violent parts of them trigger me into fury.

Sometimes I want to give up on you, Earth, and enjoy myself instead – less world-on-my-shoulders worrying, less weighty responsibility, less care. More detective films, more tourism, more chocolate cake, more money, more stuff.

What can I do? What is the secret to everything?

I can relax my frightened heart, and let a little more love through.

I can remember that none of us really know what we're doing or what effects we'll have. I can let kindness cover your wound like gauze, darling Earth, because love is always bigger than darkness. I can forgive the parts of me that struggle to love some parts of other people, and let you love them instead. I can look fondly at my pleasure-seeking impulses, and the protective parts of me that try to avoid pain, and make space for all of it. I can choose responsibility *and* chocolate cake.

I can let your love trickle into me. I can let the stars and the squirrels show me the way. I can crumple softly in recognition before the dark spiky knots in others. I can bathe all my soreness in light.

I can lean into your lap, dear Earth, as your lap is soft
and wide.

I can lean into your lap, dear Earth, as your lap is soft
and wide.

Love, Satya

Dear Earth, the birds are happy

After months of procrastinating I finally ordered the sacks of seed, moved the bird feeder station from where weeds were strangling it, and filled the tubes with fat balls, sunflower hearts and niger. This morning the word is starting to get out and birds are coming for their breakfast.

If I was going to rate my general efficiency, lovely Earth, I would give myself 93%. I do the things I say I'm going to do, and I get them done fast. I do my self-assessment tax return on the first day I'm allowed to. I'm one of those people. However, there are black spots. If you looked at the horror that is the inside of my car, or opened the cupboard in the hallway, you'd see a different story.

Certain tasks on my to-do list develop a force-field of resistance around them. The longer this force-field is active, the stronger it gets. These tasks often have a physical element – I have very little faith in my body – and they take up continuous space in my head even though I try my best to ignore them.

We all have black spots. Some people have force-fields around maths, or feeling their feelings, or saying sorry. In the past, I would approach my own black spots as a challenge – how can I improve this part of me? What structures can I put in place to support that growth? How can I work hard and become perfect at this?

These days, I accept that I will never be entirely free of them. They might shift about, but it's impossible to self-improve them all away. I have strengths, which sometimes flip over into weaknesses – my over-efficiency means I miss out on playing. Here are my weaknesses, which sometimes flip over into strengths – my avoidance of physical work means I retreated into books and became a writer.

Darling Earth, it feels better to live this way – with a deep frank acknowledgement of my fallibilities, my quirks and my annoyances. It helps me to shove myself less often – because no-one enjoys being shoved and it's often counter-productive. It helps me to be gentle with the black spots of others. It helps me to remember the value of community, where we help our friend who isn't great at maths with their taxes and they help us by mowing our lawn.

We are connected to each other and to you, dear Earth, by our failings more than by our successes. That's where the opportunity is – that's where the sweet spots are. When we can welcome these soft spots, and let others help us, we become whole and golden.

I put the birdseed out late this year, and the birds ate elsewhere or maybe went hungry. I am sorry, birds. And, here you are – feasting, sparking with beauty, happy.

Love, Satya

Dear Earth, I get so angry at climate deniers

I'm not usually an angry person. I can live and let live. And, when people tell me that the facts of global heating or the dying coral are confected conspiracy, darling Earth, I get so angry that I don't know what to do about it.

I am curious about what is going on for me. I understand that, from where they're standing, what they believe not only makes sense but is necessary for their worldview to remain intact. I get that, if they are wholly certain of their rightness, then there is no point in spending time in debate. I see the small part of me that is confused by their inviolable conviction, and begins to wonder, 'have I got this all terribly wrong?' I get that a large part of my identity is invested in my being an earth protector, and so feel that they are accusing me of stupidity.

None of this entirely explains my anger. The anger is the anger of a mother bear protecting her cubs.

Yes, that's it. I see them as threatening you, fragile Earth. Of threatening the slow progress we are making in getting the facts out through a biased media. Of threatening the necessary shifting of public opinion to effect huge systemic change. I see them as attacking you, as if they were themselves going into the Amazon, slashing and burning. As if they themselves were flooding your rivers with poison or sucking all richness from your soil.

'They'. 'Them'. Ah, the familiar comforts of being on the 'right' side of history. Of being the goody, and of knowing who the baddies are.

Of course, there is no 'them'. There is just us. Some of us are lost in preoccupation with survival, and we can't rely on them to help us – how could they? Some of us are convinced that this emergency is a conspiracy, and we shouldn't rely on them to help us – why would they?

Some of us were born lucky, dear Earth, and we can see that you urgently need our help. Once we see this, it is our duty (our grievous burden, our privilege, our joy) to do what we can.

I can bow to my fierce anger when it arises, and try to protect others from the fire of it, whilst transmuting as much of it as I can into right action.

I can bow to the climate deniers. I can respect that their opinions have integrity for them, from where they're standing, and utterly disagree with them – without needing them to change their minds. I can remember that they love and are loved.

I can bow to you, dear Earth. My love for you is fierce. I think you love me like this too – I think your love is big enough for us all.

Love, Satya

Dear Earth, forgive me for using you as a mirror

We humans are experts at using objects as extensions of our precious selves.

I look in my wallet and I think, 'new gloves for me'. I look at my cat and I think, 'purr for me'. I glance at your autumn colours, a procession of fiery finery, and think, 'cold out, a cosy evening inside for me'.

This turning of all objects into our personal mirrors can be subtle, insidious. If I'm not careful, even my offerings to the world become mere signposts back to me. My writing is manufactured to receive praise, rather than being an attempt at expressing the beckoning ineffable. My running the temple becomes focused on growing a congregation around me, rather than giving away the brightest jewels I've received.

I know you don't mind too much, dear Earth. And, I know that whenever I look through my 'me-glasses', I miss out. I miss out on the wild Otherness of you. I miss out on the messages you have for me. I miss out on the 'drunkenness of things being various'.

It doesn't help when I scold myself for turning everything into the Satya show. What helps is noticing when I'm doing it, and then shifting my gaze just a teensy bit. I can imagine your gentle hand under my chin, darling Earth, showing me your exquisite detail. The flick-tailed wren sheltering in the bush. The honest clean taste of turnips. The wisdom of lakes.

I am blessed, dear Earth, by your continued invitation into a deeper relationship with you. You are so much richer than a mirror. When I open my senses to your music, beloved, I forget how I look and I *dance*.

Love, Satya

Dear Earth, thank you for little dogs

I'm not a natural walker. As a child I couldn't see the point of walking unless there was something good at the end of it – a playground, or maybe a sweet shop. I hoped that getting a dog would encourage me from your buildings, Earth, and out under the high ceilings of your skies.

Our little dog Aiko doesn't need much walking – she's satisfied with one outing a day. She's already been walked today by her uncle Dayamay. When I received the gift of an unexpected hour this afternoon, I was surprised to hear myself think, 'I could take her out for a quick turn around the block'.

There is a short loop from the temple which takes us along the main road, up a quiet residential street studded with big quirky houses I lust after, down a short grassy corridor, down the hill and back along the main street. It doesn't take more than twenty minutes.

After our walk, my brain feels like a shaken-out rug. There is a little more space between the cells in my body.

Aiko has proved to be a good getting-me-outside device. There are others – vegetable patches, cameras, friends, and slices of cake with a walk to get to them. I am grateful for these devices, as they remind me to look up at the sliver of moon and down at the green straggles of weeds dotting the pavements. They give me an excuse to have a conversation with you, beloved Earth. This time is never wasted.

Little dog is napping, and I have some more work to do before the day is done. I'll carry your influence with me, airy Earth, like cloth soaked in sweet incense smoke.

Love, Satya

Dear Earth, I had a little meltdown

Today I had the whole morning free to work on writing my new e-course. I began by setting up the mechanics of the automated emails. I encountered a technical problem, and then another, and then another. Over the course of an hour, then two, a tangled knot formed in my stomach and tightened and tightened. Eventually it fulminated into bitter tears.

After the intensity eased, and with the help of my kind husband, I became curious about what I was so upset about. I know that sorting out the tech can take ages, so which part of me had thrown itself onto the floor in anguished overwhelm?

I found it. It was the part of me that writes. My writing part has been squeezed into the edges of my too-busy life for months. I listened to it. It told me it had enjoyed getting up in the middle of the night to write these letters to you, darling Earth, but that it missed having proper swathes of time in my week. I had promised that it would have a whole morning to write, it told me, and here I was faffing about with boring plug-ins.

It pushed me to tears because it didn't know how else to get my attention. I have ignored it as I busied myself with other Good Things To Do. I'm sorry it had to shout, but I'm glad it did. Now I can make amends.

Dear Earth, I vow to listen to all the different parts of me. When I do listen, they help me to help you. They show me what my unique contribution is, and they show me how to sustain myself over the longer term. As you know, darling Earth, it's going to take a long time to put things right.

I have blocked out writing spaces in my diary and marked them with hearts. My writer is happy.

Love, Satya

Dear Earth, I made peanut butter cookies

The recipe is saved on my computer as 'yummy cookies'. They contain a high percentage of peanut butter, and so the biscuit is short in a way that I miss as a vegan – crumbly and rich and delicious. And generously studded with chocolate chunks, of course.

After they emerged from the oven and I'd tested three or four to make sure they'd come out okay, I thought, 'I'd love to share the recipe with everyone'. When we are happy and we feel safe and we have something nice, the urge to share arises naturally.

I felt a moment's smugness. What a nice person I am. And then I wondered how I'd feel if people started turning up at the temple and wanting an actual cookie. I'd be very happy to give away the first five or ten. But if a long queue formed at the door, then I'd begin to have some different feelings...

In some areas of my life I find generosity easy. In others I find it very difficult indeed. We are all different, and we all make use of people, places and things in various ways to support our impermanent egos. When these uses become threatened, our whole identities can wobble.

Dear Earth, when we consider making changes so we can live more lightly on you, we will all have very different feelings about different changes. Some people will find it easy to cut back on meat or give up flying. Others will have all sorts of security or comfort investments in pork pies, or Mediterranean family holidays. When I fall into judging others, it helps me to remember how hard it would be for me to give all my cookies away.

How can I become more generous? By letting you love me, darling Earth. And maybe I need to bake bigger batches of cookies...

Love, Satya

Dear Earth, this morning I was woken by death

He came in the form of our cat Fatty, yelling for his breakfast. He gained his silly nickname more than two decades ago, when the vet told us he was a bit too pudgy as a kitten. It's become ironic, as he's now a bag of bones. He's on four kinds of medication. He's completely deaf, his back legs are splayed, and his long hair mats so we have to shave clumps of it from him, leaving untidy white patches of skin.

I feel a faint sense of unease when I stroke him. I don't like that I can count every bone along his back. I am too aware of the end he's carrying, like a pregnancy. How many days does he have? How will it happen?

Last night we hosted a talk about your health here at the temple, dear Earth, and Fatty joined us. As I listened to the horror story for the third time, I felt more grief than I've felt before. My ears wanted to close up before the stories of suffering. I baulked at contemplating our dark future.

You will die one day too, of course, beloved Earth. Whether we'll cause our own extinction or not isn't your main preoccupation, as you've been here for a long time before we arrived and you'll be around for a long time after us. With death ahead of us, as a planet, as a species and as individuals, how should we live?

I do want to live. I want to feel the grief as well as the joy. I want to acknowledge the parts of me that shy away from Fatty's bony back, and from hearing the reality about the climate and ecological crisis. I want to be kind to these parts of me, and give them a hug. There will be dying, and here is a whole day ahead of me. Outside the pale green catkins are bobbing in the breeze next to the spent anemones, with their branching bobble-tipped seed heads. There are bright splashes of tangerine nasturtiums in the spent vegetable patch. What abundance!

Towards the end of the talk I left my chair to sit on the ground next to Fatty. I rubbed his cheeks and stroked his head, and he purred and purred.

With so much aching love, Satya

Dear Earth, let's practice praising

Let's praise the woman who upset me yesterday, for showing me a corner of myself which is bitter and hurting, and which needs more soft attention.

Let's praise the battered stalks of kale, stripped naked up to their shoulders, for having spared us some leaves after plumping up several armies of caterpillars.

Let's praise the horrible stink of meat in this vegan household which gives our cats life, and the succession of purring visitors who woke me in the night to demand strokes.

Let's praise the head cold which reminds us how it is to breathe, and which lays us down gently on the verges of our frantic days for a while.

Let's praise the man who told me your coral reefs aren't dying, dear Earth, but flourishing – for showing me how fierce my love for you is. So fierce, it frightens me.

Let's praise the dying that makes room for bright shoots. Let's praise the scientists who are bringing us terrible news. Let's praise the concrete cities that mirror our best and our worst. Let's praise the grief that scours us into luminosity.

Let's see how far our radical praise will reach into the darkness, dear Earth. See how it transforms the ugliest monsters. See how it asks us to expand our bruised hearts. See how it graces us with a bottomless faith.

With gratitude and love, Satya

Dear Earth, it's the simple things

Yesterday we had a very simple day. We woke late in a leisurely fashion, went for a long walk with Aiko, ate a vegan fry-up for lunch, napped, read our books, did a little bit of writing, and had a pizza-and-television evening.

I remember several times thinking, 'I am happy'. It wasn't because of anything complicated, darling Earth. I was happy to spot a heron gazing out across the pond. I was happy to eat a bowl of Ben & Jerry's caramel coconut ice-cream. I was happy to read my novel about trees. These ordinary things felt like extraordinary luxuries yesterday, dear Earth, because they are.

What luxury to have a whole day off to walk through the woods and across the fields in bright November sunshine. What luxury to have a husband who loves me. What luxury to have my health. What extravagant, preposterous luxury to be alive in these times, in this country, in this body, right now.

Today I'm burrowing back into work, and picking up complicated threads of correspondence and lists of things to do. I'm still carrying yesterday's glow, and it's also slipping through my fingers. Our brains contain universes, and many of our protective habits keep us from experiencing you as I did yesterday, sweet Earth.

That's okay. Whether I feel the glow or not, I know it's there. Parts of me remember how lucky I am, even when other parts of me are flooding me with their pain, hunger or despair. The sun is always there, despite dark clouds.

Love, Satya

Dear Earth, is deep change possible?

I spent many happy years in 'the rooms' – twelve step programmes like Alcoholics Anonymous which help people to manage their unmanageable compulsions. I especially loved the group that meets at the Buddhafield festival, where those of us with different addictions come together and find out what we have in common. That, it turns out, is a lot.

I spent many hours in those church halls and grimy community centres listening to people who had no hope. I'm on the 'controlling' side of the addict-codependent spectrum, and so my own dysfunction has taken the form of over-functioning. From the outside I generally look pretty sorted! Others in these rooms just so happened to be on the other side of that spectrum and lived lives that included life-threatening drug addictions, violence, abuse, removal of children, prison and long stretches in mental health hospitals. I've listened to victims and perpetrators, the abused and abusers, and heard of many whose addictions have claimed them.

There by the grace of God. I am under no illusions about my specialness or cleverness in avoiding these fates. The accident of birth into my particular family, in this country, in these times, has gifted me amazing privilege. Many are not so lucky.

What does all this have to do with you, dear Earth? Well, humanity has messed up, and we have messed up big time. Our systems are strangling you, and sometimes I feel that the necessary big change is impossible.

I also thought that it was impossible to come back from the deep hell of addiction. I understand how a person's whole identity, their whole way of being, can rest on a substance that is killing them. I am aware of the bleakness of the recovery statistics, and I am familiar with relapse.

And. I have seen miracles. I have met a smiling healthy suited man who showed me a photo of his previous self, homeless and near death. I have heard murderers speak of thirty years of sobriety and service to others. I have seen wounded men and women allowing the love of their fellows to trickle into the cracks of their magnificent defences.

I have seen dead women get up and walk, and kindness blooming in the darkest hellish pits of the human psyche.

We are in need of some miracles. The rich are addicted to their money and their power, and giving it up will be near impossible. We have our own addictions which are contributing to your pain, Earth. We are foolish beings.

Near impossible. People go to the twelve step rooms to find hope when they have none. Sometimes they find it. We need new stories, of how a vegan sausage roll saved a high street bakery and turned its owner vegan. Of how a film star decided to be arrested in Earth's name every Friday. Of how a populist national newspaper dedicated a whole issue to the climate crisis. Of how sixteen year olds and ninety one year olds glued themselves to you and were carried off by the police because they loved you, dear Earth. Because they love you.

I believe in miracles, darling Earth.

Love, Satya

Dear Earth, please help me to ask for help

Beloved Earth, I am terrible at asking for help. When others help me I feel vulnerable, a nuisance, in their debt, and a failure.

My culture has taught me to worship self-sufficiency. "What a clever girl – you've done it all by yourself." "If you want something done properly..." I was a good student, and I have become a master. Self-sufficiency keeps us safe!

And, self-sufficiency takes a weighty toll. My needs sometimes build up and then splurge out in my marriage, in an emotional *bleaugh*. Sometimes my body makes me ill as a last resort to opt me out for a while. I am deprived of the richness of other's input, as I think I know the best way to do everything. I miss out on being-with.

I respect the parts of me that keep me safe in this way. They're protecting me from being rejected, resented or pitied. They have good reasons for keeping help out. The change happens as I notice when I shut down, and send kindness to the frightened parts of me. The change happens as I experiment in safe ways – asking a friend for a lift to the vet, or receiving a small offered thing. The change happens as I learn to say a firm 'no' when I am asked for something that is beyond me. The change happens as I watch and learn from others.

Beloved Earth, I am learning to ask for help. When others help me, parts of me still sometimes feel vulnerable, a nuisance, in their debt, and a failure. I also feel nicely-surprised, connected, abundant, grateful, tender, blessed, and happy.

You are so good at it, darling Earth. Look at your soil, your creatures, your weather, your ecosystems! The intimacy of your giving and receiving! The festival of symbiosis and abundance!

Please help me to open my heart, dear Earth. Please help me to give you the gift of being received.

Lots of love, Satya

Dear Earth, I finally washed my robes

Since my arrest at the rebellion, my red and yellow robes have been splattered in dried mud. I've worn them for our three weekly Buddhist services here at the temple, catching sight of the dirt and grime as I circumambulate our golden Buddha and bow to the floor.

I'm a lazy house-keeper, but even so I'm curious about what took me so long to clean them. Why have I been clinging to that mud?

I felt like I was in battle for you in London, beloved Earth. I want to avoid war metaphors, as we are rising up in peace and we hold non-violence as our beacon. And, I felt like I was on the front line. Those around me made stunning sacrifices for you, dear Earth. We lined up against the police, and we held on for as long as we could.

I'm not on the front line now, as I write this letter in the hope that it may help others to help you. The grief I carry for you is strong, and parts of me try to assuage it by getting me to do more, do more. I can never do enough, but when I was there on the streets, surrounded by my comrades, I at least felt useful and alive.

I know that we need mud and blood to help you, dear Earth. We also need words and rest and donations and conversations and placard-painting and praying and e-courses and baking peanut cookies to keep us all going.

I think some of us also need Buddhist services, and my clean robes will help me to lead an hour of practice tonight.

I hear the part of me that is desperate for me to do more. 'Leave the temple! Sit outside Parliament until they listen to you!' I get it. I hear the part of me that is grieving, and that sees further damage to you unfolding even as I type. I'm sending these parts of me love.

Love multiplies. As this love sinks in, through my robes, into my bones, it also radiates out. Can you feel it?

Love, Satya

Dear Earth, help me to stop reading the news

I am being pulled in a thousand tiny directions.

The election. Brexit. Impeachment. He said. She said. What I think about what he said. What they think about what he said. And the Amazon is still burning.

Keeping up to date with these tiny details is an attempt at feeling less afraid, less out of control. Maybe if I know everything, I could prepare for what's coming. Maybe I could do the single right thing that would save the world.

Dear Earth, I don't think you fret over the details. You know that it took millennia to make this lump of flint, this fragrant rose. You know that the most sustainable kind of change is slow change. You know that this snail, this patch of earth, this magnolia tree, are all playing their appropriate part in this cosmic play.

Beloved Earth, help me to remember your glacial ease. If I take my eye off the cacophonous torrent of news, I won't become unsafe. If I watch the bird-feeder for a while, this coal tit stuffing his beak with suet, this gaudy magpie swaggering across the veg patch, I won't miss out. The opposite.

Help me to see what role you've cast me in, dear Earth – not the director, just Satya – with writing to do, cats to feed, and dirty dishes to wash. It's a wonderful role and, when I stick to my own lines, it's perfect for me. It's enough.

I'm enough. And so are we all.

Love, Satya

Dear Earth, the weather inside my head is gloomy

Nothing particular has happened. A series of irritations, an underlying grief, a couple of triggers. Weariness after weeks of work. A backlog of bitterness that has burst like a spot. Weather is complicated, both on your body and inside my head, dear Earth.

As complex as they are, we can change entire weather systems. We already have. I don't have to tell you about the carbon dioxide, darling Earth.

What helps my weather system? Putting myself in good conditions – eating Buddha bowls, doing spiritual practice, sharing with other humans, rest. Eating art, and going on walks to look at your goldfinches and at your million greens. The usual stuff.

What also helps is remembering that I'm not in control of the entire thing. My internal weather system leans on genes, your weather, early childhood experience, my loved one's internal weather, my old cat's health, Brexit...

I'm not the God of my weather. God is God. Earth, despite your astonishing talent for balancing yourself, you are also at the mercy of the creatures that live on you, and of Brother Sun, and of the Universe.

There are things that we can do, and then we may as well surrender. Today the weather inside my head is gloomy. That's okay. It'll lighten again, before too long.

In the meantime, I can praise you, beloved Earth. Your moth-eaten yellow magnolia leaves just clinging onto their twigs. Your huge sunflower head, left for the birds and now with a bloom of ash-grey mould. Your mud brought in on paws. Your blurred landscape behind the endless rain. What gloomy beauty!

Always yours, Satya

Dear Earth, what dance shall we do today?

It's miserable out. My body is thick with an impending cold. Right now, I feel like a useless hulk of flesh. I want to go back to bed and hide.

A question keeps arising in me – what can I offer today? I don't want to ask this question. I want to ask 'what can I receive today?' And still the other question insists on itself, a song thrush repeating its call.

Okay, let's try. Today I can offer my care and attention to my psychotherapy clients. Hmm. As I write that, there's a small easing somewhere. What else feels do-able? I can reply to two waiting letters from friends. Yes, that would be a nice thing to do, maybe even from bed. I'll enjoy that and so will they. What else? I'll dance the usual essential errands of a house-holder – breakfast for the animals and me, taking out the rubbish... but slower than usual. Slowly and with kindness to myself.

Do I have energy for anything else? No – that feels enough for today. Maybe I'll read some more of 'Braiding Sweetgrass'. Maybe I'll eat some vegan fudge. Maybe later some fresh energy will arise like a bubbling spring, and maybe not.

Now I've decided on my offering, something is suddenly clear. You don't need me to do anything, darling Earth, in order for me to receive your care. You'll offer me your luscious fruits and nourishing grains whether or not I'm useful. You'll ply me with oxygen, and play me the music of rustling leaves.

You know that I'll feel better if I twirl in your arms, and that making some small offering is a way for me to step onto the dance floor. You know about the burden of guilt I carry, for not doing enough – for not being enough. You know how to help me with it. Once I start dancing, I almost forget it.

I'll make a cup of tea now, and wake the little dog. She'll stretch luxuriously and then her tail will start going, in her delight at another day, in her delight at my ordinary face. I'll rub her flank and her soft pink belly, and she'll roll over in bliss. After writing you these words, that will be a good start to today's gentle dance.

With so much love, Satya

Dear Earth, I am boring

I am forty five years old. For decades now, I have written about how we can accept ourselves. For decades, I have lost myself in computers and overwork. For decades, I have liked the same things – cats, words, chocolate – and disliked the same things – fairground rides, cleaning, secrets.

Sometimes I yearn to be a phoenix, and to burn through all that old wood.

And, old wood is precious. It holds everything up and, as it gently rots, it provides the sustenance for new life.

This lifetime, I get to be a Satya tree. I don't get to be a George tree or a Polly tree. As much as I sometimes envy other trees, I don't think I'd want to be them if it came down to it. I'd miss these creaky old branches. I'm just about getting to know what this tree needs, and what it is capable of. I'm just beginning to get to know cats and words and I definitely haven't eaten enough chocolate yet.

I'm deeply in love with 'Bill is Dead' at the moment, a song by The Fall – I play it over and over. I loved Mark E. Smith. He was an irascible alcoholic, full of intelligence, spite and genius. I don't love him despite these qualities, but with them. I think it's what makes his music so brilliant. It isn't always pretty. It's real.

I'm at peace with being boring. I get to be this particular tree for, if I'm lucky, a few more decades. And, of course, miracles have happened right here. I am the same old tree, and I have been transformed beyond recognition after a lifetime of weather and grace. There have been surprises, and I'm sure there'll be more. I'm not just a cat person – I'm a dog person too! I got arrested for activism! I married a Buddhist monk! I run a Buddhist temple! Who'd have thought it?

Dear Earth, thank you for keeping me watered and fed and for growing me. Thank you for my fellows, for all the other animals, and for your green magnificence. I'll do my best to produce the fruit I was born to produce. I'll do my best to enjoy it all. These are the greatest times of my life.

With much love, Satya

Dear Earth, let's talk about politics

What do politics have do with you, darling Earth? The false promises, the stinking lies, the manipulation, the undignified jockeying for power. Why invest my time and energy into all that when I could be out planting trees?

Politics are "the activities associated with the governance of a country or area, especially the debate between parties having power." Here's the rub. These people are the ones who can save you, dear Earth, or continue hurrying you towards despoliation and chaos.

I must confess that I've never had an appetite for politics. Parts of me find it unsafe to be around such intricate spinning, and I have traditionally dealt with that by washing my hands of the lot of them.

Two things have changed. The first is that, as I've got older, I've met the parts of me that intricately spin, and the parts of me that grab at power, and I feel less like a different species to those I see on the screens. I also know more about how it is when you begin to move in those circles – how the rules are different, and how difficult it is not to be changed into a worse version of yourself in order to survive. Many of us want our politicians to be reassuring, not human. We want to feel safe, and so in some ways they are expected to play the role of 'mummy and daddy'. They have their own reasons for stepping forward – a mix, I'm sure, of altruistic and selfish intentions – and, they also carry a lot for us all.

The second is that I have heard your distress, sweet Earth. It's not about my preference to opt out any more, it's about my responsibility to you.

On Saturday, after twenty four hours of Buddhist chanting for you, I will walk the streets of Malvern with my friends, our faces painted as skulls. We will be urging the people of our small town to ask our local election candidates about their approach to your crisis, beloved Earth. Others will attend the hustings. I will use my vote for you. With this piece of writing, I am encouraging others to do the same.

Politics is a complicated and messy business, just like all the other things that happen on your lap, dear Earth. What can we do? We can be a part of it. We can demand the truth. We can vote. We can become political in our own little spheres, and try to do what is best for our fellows. We can support our politicians and remember that they are human. We can role-model dignity, and stop ourselves from putting others down as a way of propping ourselves up. We can feel our disappointment, rage and grief in the face of human greed, hate and delusion.

We can remember our love for you, dear Earth, and let it guide us.

Love, Satya

Dear Earth, I hear it

Yesterday I was feeling physically low and so I rested at home. In the afternoon I walked around the temple garden, which I have neglected.

The spent hydrangea pom-poms were holding their rich dusky pink. The pyracantha's berries have turned firebox red, and hang in clumps like tiny grapes. The pond is clotted with hairy weed and as we passed Aiko bent to lap at the cold surface.

I sat on our platform on a wooden chair with peeling paint, Aiko beside me, and the late November sun pelted us. A pocket of peace. I happened to glance behind me and caught a shape moving in the dark corners of the hedge – a wren!

Speaking with a friend this week, I was touched to hear her describe my writing as 'a call to beauty'. The phrase has stayed with me. So many of us – gardeners, artists, cooks – do variations of this work. And, of course, you are the master of calling us to beauty, beloved Earth. How could I ever compete with this huge decaying blossom, this tangled pond, the jaunty tail of this tiny honeycomb-boned creature?

I hear your call of beauty. I am asked to linger, the sun on my face. I am called to worship these eight goldfinches. I am compelled to do what I can to protect you. I am called to record fragments of your riches, and to offer these words as gifts.

With love, dear Earth. Satya

Dear Earth, we stayed up all night for you

Did you hear us? We filled the room with our voices and we circled the sacred shrine we made for you, with a globe and a sprig of green alkanet and a scarlet autumn leaf.

Sometimes it still strikes me as a very strange thing to do. Why spend a whole night walking in circles, singing the same phrase over and over? Wouldn't that time be better used if we protested or were political or worked on the land? How are we helping you?

As I chanted, I was opening myself to the love of the Buddhas. This is the love that held me as the police arrested me and lifted me from the road. This is the love that moves me to fill the bird feeder. This is the love that taps me on the shoulder when I encounter the worst of myself or of others, and reminds me that we are all doing our best.

For me, the most reliable path to this love just happens to be chanting the nembutsu. Others have other paths, dear Earth – many of them involving you. I don't think the love minds whether you use sacred books or surfing or prayer mats or forests or twelve step groups. If we are given a tiny glimpse of our connection with something much-bigger-than-us, then hallelujah! We need this connection more than ever as you call us to help you, precious Earth. We need courage and determination and fierce care.

I was soaked in this love during my hours in the shrine room. It hasn't turned me into a new and improved version of myself, as much as I always hope it will. It did connect me with your suffering. It did connect me with your nourishing sweetness. I am complete. I am ready for whatever is next.

With much love, Satya

Dear Earth, here's to enjoying the delightful

Indigo? Sapphire? Cobalt? I'm searching for the perfect word. The sun hides behind the hills across the valley and the sky becomes saturated: such a rich, deep blue. Spotted with warm yellow lights and framing the pale speckled moon, I could gaze at it for hours.

During one of his Dharma talks this week, my Buddhist teacher encouraged us to both "be with the horrors, and enjoy the delightful." Today I want to focus on your delights, dear Earth.

What gets between us and this enjoyment? All the protective parts of us that are working so hard to keep us safe. To enjoy delights, we need to take off our thick gloves and reach out with our delicate skin. Maybe the last time we reached out for a rose, a thorn drew blood. It may be that we're reluctant to be seen. Maybe we don't feel entitled to enjoyment. Maybe we're too busy chasing success or praise.

You want us to enjoy you, darling Earth. You created the sweet fizzy goo inside passion fruits. You made the soft fur on my little dog's belly. You host Maidenhair trees and waterfalls and ice topped mountains. You are crammed with delights – snowflakes! peacock feathers! – and you offer them endlessly.

Sometimes I catch a glimpse of my gloves. I realise that I've been looking at your beauty through smeared glass. As I see and appreciate this shielding, and reassure it, it relaxes a little. As it relaxes, I feel the silk under my fingertips again, and taste the blue of the evening sky.

My prayer today is: help me to enjoy your delights, dear Earth.

Love, Satya

Dear Earth, I made you bakewell tarts

I know how you like them, with crisp pastry and a generous splodge of sticky raspberry jam. The people who come to our temple open morning will eat them for you, and enjoy them. That will make you happy.

Now I am stringing words together for you. Later I will clean out the cat litter tray for you, and put on the washing. This afternoon I will sit with four people for an hour each, and bring them healing in your name.

When I do things in the spirit of making an offering, they shine. The tarts become precious jewels. The clearing away of shit becomes a way of showing caring for our bony old cat. My work as a psychotherapist becomes sanctified, becomes a great privilege.

I forget, darling Earth. I resent the endless washing of clothes and sweeping of stairs. I feel unappreciated and weary. I bombard myself with guilt – I should be doing different things for you in your time of need, braver things, more.

Then the bakewell tarts come out of the oven, golden and begging to be eaten. I remember that I am spreading kindness. I remember that there are billions of us being kind to each other. Even the ones who are twisted and afraid, even the ones who lie and control – even they experience moments of offering clear compassion. The sun finds a way of breaking through.

There will be storms ahead. We will need as many

bakewell tarts as we can gather. I will keep making offerings, and I will keep having faith in kindness.

Much love, Satya

Dear Earth, today we are voting for our leader

I'm no political expert, but I do know people. People are selfish. People make decisions based mostly on what suits them, and on what keeps them safe – even the decisions that look to most people like altruistic ones.

A pessimistic view? I find it a realistic one, and a deeply liberating one. It gives me permission to see my own deep selfishness, and to expect this selfishness in others.

Why are we like this? Because we are astonishingly, heart-achingly vulnerable. We walk around with our everso-thin skin and a chest-full of complicated organs, dependent on your perfect mix of gases for every single breath, dear Earth.

Other humans might pierce this fragile body-bubble at any time. We also depend on other humans for our tribal sense of safety – whether we'll be sheltered by the safe arms of the group, or expelled into the wilderness to perish. Our brains are hard-wired to scan continually – who is a threat? Who do we need to keep on our side? Who might protect us?

I could go on. For me, the miracle is that in amongst this desperately-not-wanting-to-die, we are graced with moments of utter shining generosity. We open a door for a struggling mum. We give our last fiver to someone who needs it more than we do. We leap into the river to save someone else's child.

I think that you see all this, darling Earth. I think that you know how frightened we are, and how much of what we do is an attempt at shoring up our defences. I think you feel tenderly towards us. When I remember this, I feel tender towards myself, and to others.

How should we vote for our leader? By being curious. What are we afraid of? Where are the limits of our generosity? What truths are we avoiding? What dirty work do we hope our leaders will do for us? When we've acknowledged all this fear and sent love to it all, we'll be more likely to wonder about what might be best for our friends, for our enemies, for our country. For you, dear Earth.

Whatever happens next, you need us to keep speaking up on your behalf. We can't trust other selfish beings like us to get it right all the time. We need to keep using our own power, like 76 year old grandfather Peter Cole. At the time of writing he has been without food for twenty four days for your sake.

His offering is a radiant star in the night sky. When we come together our sparks of generosity become a torch, and they will light the way.

Love, Satya

Dear Earth, meet our Buddha of the car park

He came to live out the front of our temple last February, after we went on a trip to Japan and were inspired by their roadside shrines. He weighs a tonne – four strong men just about managed to rock him inch by inch from the pick-up truck to his tree stump.

Yesterday morning I sat quietly in our shrine room and watched him through the window. He was sitting where he usually does, looking out at the world. Cars swooshed past. Passers-by walked within a couple of metres of him, going from here to there. The world changed around him. He sat.

He sits, dear Earth, and beams out a message to the world. There is something more than the daily grind. There is something more than the hustle and bustle of consumerism. There is a place of peace, of rest, where we can replenish our weary hearts. There is a lap we can lean into as we re-find our steady centres.

As I watched him, my own heart settled. I took comfort from his immovability in all this impermanence. I know that his concrete body will wear away too, eventually. Even the Buddha's image will one day fade. And, what he represents will never leave us. I trust that we'll be visited by new prophets. The wise ones will say the same things as the prophets of old.

Love is bigger than anything else. We can lean into

this love, and find our courage. We can soak it up and carry it around like a brilliant flame.

From your humble servant, Satya

Dear Earth, sometimes we need naps

At the weekend I gave out leaflets to a few hundred people and was refused by a few hundred more. Twenty of my Buddhist colleagues were sitting behind me in meditation posture on the wet city pavements. We were there to encourage people to 'be kind to the Earth at Christmas', without scrimping on any of the most important ingredients – good company, thoughtfulness, relaxation, fun. I hope you were pleased to see us there, dear Earth.

Afterwards we ate together and I told my friend how utterly exhausted I was. She'd also been handing out leaflets and said she felt energised – and she guessed correctly that I was an introvert rather than an extrovert like her. Being with people drains me of energy, and it fires her up.

I wondered later if I should have chosen to be one of those sitting instead. My answer was 'no', dear Earth, because I wanted to connect with people – I wanted to offer them my beaming smile and have delicate conversations with them about your health. I was glad to be drained of energy for you.

It's good to play to our strengths. You need all our strengths, darling Earth – lawyers, hedge-layers, artists, home bakers, scientists, those who start local groups, those who do the washing up after the group has gone home.

It is also okay to do the thing that doesn't come naturally to us, knowing that it will have a cost. Sometimes it's important that we do the thing that tires us out, or that we do the thing we really don't want to do. If possible we should do these things sparingly, so as not to exhaust our system – an exhausted system is no good to anyone, least of all ourselves.

      After all that contact I slept for most of the afternoon, a little dog curled up beside me, and I woke up restored. I'll organise one of these actions again, but not for a while. First, the holidays, and a longer period of rest. Christmas is the perfect time for naps.

Much love, Satya

Dear Earth, my word for the year is...

Gentle.

The gentle of my cat's soft paw when he places it on my cheek in the mornings, patting me awake.

The gentle of tucking a sweet-pea seedling into the duvet of the earth.

The gentle of receiving sharp anger, hot jealousy and abysmal mistakes with sweet tenderness.

You know gentle, darling Earth. You know how to cosset baby birds in yolk, and how to decorate spiderwebs with gems. You know how to keep ecosystems in precise, delicate balance. You know how to grow the soft silver fur on pussy willow buds.

I want to keep learning from you. I want to recognise when parts of me shove the rest of me along – for good reasons, but with a cost. I want to keep greeting my foolishness with compassion. I want to be brutally realistic about my limits, and meet them with kindness.

I will carry this word with me like a charm as I venture into the new year. I'll need it, dear Earth, as I speak up for you with a fiercer love than ever.

(Reader – what will your word be?)

Much love, Satya

Dear Earth, help me to give up resolutions

I've always been a sucker for self-improvement schemes. I am convinced that if only I was more disciplined, a tad more famous, a little bit thinner (etc.) that life would be perfect. This means that I get very strong urges to better myself, especially at this time of year.

There's nothing wrong with aspirations. If I didn't have aspirations, I wouldn't have done many of the good things I've done – written books, created a temple, trained as a psychotherapist. What's unhelpful is thinking that a new and improved version of Satya would be happier or, more crucially, more lovable.

When I look into the eyes of my dog Aiko, darling Earth, I see her adoring me. She doesn't care if I'm sixty or eighty kilograms. She doesn't care if I've written five books or a hundred or none. She doesn't care how many religious texts I've read before breakfast or how many people liked my last Facebook post.

She does like it when I rub her neck. She does like it when I smile back at her, and when I'm happy.

I do have plans for this year. I do want to finish a book for you, dear Earth, and to re-start a modest yoga practice after a lapsed year.

As I say this, I acknowledge the self-improvement-nut parts of me that get immediately excited. 'Ooh, yoga will tone your flabby body and then you'll be beautiful! Ooh, the book will make you really popular!' I'm reminding these parts that I find the process of doing yoga and writing worthwhile, and that's enough. The results are irrelevant, because I am already loved just as I am.

Look into those doggie eyes. Just as I am – this is how Aiko loves me. And this is how you love me too, dear Earth.

With gratitude, Satya

Dear Earth, what six things do you need from us?

One. You need us to enjoy you. You need us to lean into your soft brilliant mosses and watch the flamingo-pink cyclamen pirouette up from your dark skin. You need us to be wowed by your star-blanket and your talking trees and your luminous deep sea creatures. You need us to know that your raindrops on our cheeks are kisses.

Two. You need us to raise the alarm – to wade upstream against the raging current of our broken systems. You need us to speak up clearly and loudly to our governments and to big corporations and to all the parts of people that are strangling you for profit and power. You need us to say NO.

Three. You need us to be changed by you. You need us to listen and learn from indigenous peoples, to remember what our ancient ancestors knew, and to live lightly and gratefully on your lap. You need us to choose wisely. You need us to say please and thank you, and to only take as much as we need.

Four. You need us to shine our fierce kindness towards ourselves – the parts that despair, the parts that despise, the parts that want to solve this by dividing us into good guys and bad guys. You need us to work towards healing the young parts of us that were abandoned or abused, because this work helps everyone.

Five. You need us to keep our eyes and ears open to your pain. If we are safe enough, you need us to allow the grief to rise up, bitter and heavy. Our grief is our most precious resource in our sacred work for you. You need us to know this in our bones, and to pass this knowledge on.

Six. You need us to care for you, sweet darling Earth, as we would our own astonishing, shining baby.

With all of me, Satya

Dear Earth, gently does it

Today is the last day of holiday before work begins again. As usual, parts of me have ambitious plans for the year. Become super-rich-and-famous, single-handedly save the world – that kind of thing.

My word for this year has been travelling with me – a constant companion in a way no previous word has been. It crouches delicately on my shoulder, a soft-feathered thing with big liquid eyes, and every so often it whispers into my ear. Gentle. Gentle. Even the word itself is a caress of sibilance.

'I'll lose weight and become a better role-model of a vegan.' Gentle. 'I'll squeeze in volunteering a day a week for Extinction Rebellion.' Gentle. 'I'll become a better cleaner and keep my currently-disgusting car spotless.' Gentle.

I am making a change. I've chosen one thing – the thing that disrupts my everyday life the most – my unhealthy use of the internet. I've asked for help. I've joined a twelve step group and have set some realistic bottom lines. I've checked it out with the different parts of me, and there's general agreement that they're ready to give it a try.

For now, this change is enough. Even this change isn't in my hands – it's up to my Higher Power. This is a great relief. My life goes much better when I stop my constant conniving and manipulating, and hand it over.

Right now, I'm grateful for my new £3 mug from the supermarket with its canary yellow stripe. Right now, I'm grateful that my trousers still just-about fit. Right now, I'm grateful that you support me, dear Earth, in a million myriad ways.

The strange creature on my shoulder is whispering again... Shhhh, listen, can you hear it too?

With love, Satya

Dear Earth, I am not the forest

From here I can see the buds on the naked magnolia tree. They tip every branch like a frozen flame – silvery white, small, quiet. Each of them is busy gestating a single bloom.

I'd love to be the whole tree. I'd love to exude all that sweet perfume. I'd love to be frothy with flowers and feed all those honeybees. I'd love to shower beauty on all those around me.

Even better, I'd love to be the forest. I could be alder and copper beech, rowan and oak. I could be deadwood for mysterious fungi and branches for squirrels to dance along. I could be basket canes, blackberries, medicine, pointy-noised shrews. I could exhale clouds of oxygen and hug all that carbon close.

I'm not the forest. I'm just one little bud, pregnant with petals. Maybe they'll be white shreds like Magnolia stellata, or maybe they'll blush gold like 'Sunsation'. Maybe this year the frost will get to me and I'll wither. That's okay. I'm not the only one blossoming.

Dear Earth, thank you for the reminder that I only have to do my portion. Thank you also for reminding me that this little bud is made of the same stuff as waterfalls, wildebeests and thirty-metre whales. Together, we are magnificent.

Love, Satya

Dear Earth, we tie ourselves in knots

We have a furry blanket to snuggle under when watching TV, and when it's not over our knees we fold it and balance it on the back of the sofa. Roshi, our tortoiseshell and white cat, has deemed this a fine (if precarious) place for a morning nap.

I watch him sleep and I think of butterflies, charging up by spreading their wings and basking in sunshine. This reminds me of water, finding the gentlest path from A to B. This reminds me of carrot peelings becoming compost.

You show us how to find the easy route, dear Earth. You don't want us to tie ourselves in elaborate knots. What is the most important thing today? Where can we scatter a little kindness? What simple thing is asking to be done next? Taking out the rubbish? Some boring admin? Throwing a toy for the dog?

There will be suffering. There will be tasks that call for fierce courage. We are limited, and frail. We can trust that the water in our bodies will show us the easiest way to approach them – if we allow ourselves to be guided by something bigger than us, something a bit like gravity. And when furry blankets appear, we can sink right in and close our eyes. Just for a minute or two.

Love, Satya

Dear Earth, why bother?

This morning I gave a talk here at the temple called 'Introduction to Buddhism: Why Bother?' In it I explained why I (sometimes) prioritise spiritual practice over watching Netflix.

Life is often a whole lot of bother. Most of us are already stretched. It would be better for you, dear Earth, if I made my own oat milk from scratch and gave up my car and planted trees in my spare time – but that ain't happening.

The reality is that I only have a limited amount of wiggle room when it comes to extra bother, even if the extra bother would be an excellent thing to do. This is why, when I have a little capacity, I try to choose things that nourish me and that will increase my capacity further. Five minutes of spiritual practice, or a conversation with a good friend, or a dog walk in the rain.

When we go to the bother of digging out our waterproof trousers or going to a strange temple for an introductory talk, we are turning towards kindness. Kindness nourishes us and makes us healthier and happier. When we are healthier and happier, gratitude arises in us like bubbles in lemonade.

You have given us so much to be grateful for, beloved Earth. When these gratitude bubbles arise, how could we not include your birdsong and plump butternut squashes and wild prairies and the scent of ground coffee? When we experience this gratitude, how can we not want to offer you gifts in return? How can we not want to help heal you?

The first truth of Buddhism is that there is no avoiding bother. What we can do is face the bother head-on, and move as far as we are able in the direction of kindness. If there's only a millimetre of wiggle room, wonderful. A whole millimetre! What are you going to choose?

Much love, Satya

Dear Earth, I was awake in the night

After a fiery conversation I lay awake with my brain fizzing until 3 a.m. Thoughts and feelings flooded me, including raging internal debates over whether I was safe, and whether I was a good or a terrible person. It wasn't the fault of the other person – I was a gun on a hair-trigger. Like all of us, I am complex, and I have many parts. This morning they've all settled down again, but in the night there was nothing I could do to soothe them.

If I am this complex, precious Earth, and this delicate, then how much more so are you? How can the scientists even begin to make sense of what we are doing to you? I do know that they are heaping up evidence of feedback loops – one terrible snooker ball hitting another and another – and the predictions are getting scarier...

"The Earth is a huge interlinked system with different parts that all interact with and affect one another. Therefore, to try to understand the full implications of climate change and biodiversity loss, we need to think holistically. Moreover, it is unrealistic and hubristic to suppose that such holistic thinking could ever be complete or enough. We must accept living in a world that we will never fully understand. The unbelievable complexity of Earth is something before which we should be humble." ~ Extinction Rebellion: The Emergency

It's been relatively easy to return my system to equilibrium. Some writing in my journal at 1 a.m., a gentle start to the morning, an apology. An acknowledgement that I'll never 'fix' myself, just keep on making adjustments to the system. A grateful leaning in to Something Bigger, which holds me.

How can we even begin to heal you, dear Earth?

I hear her whispering: start where you are. Keep your eyes open to what is happening. Be gentle to me whenever you can. Speak up for me. Stay humble. Keep on leaning into my lap which, even as you hurt me, is wide and soft and full of love.

With sweet grief for you, Satya

Dear Earth, I woke to a dance

Our little dog was poorly last night, and so for the second time this week I counted the hours until morning.

"And?" I hear new mothers and insomniacs ask. I salute all those who manage to function on little sleep. I am feeble when it comes to needing decent chunks of it, and sleeplessness leaves me feeling under-resourced and a little panicky.

The cats kicked me out of bed just after seven, and I went into my office. I was greeted by the dark duvet of your skirts, dear Earth, jewelled with street lamps and the swoosh of car headlights. Brother Sun was shining a gentle light into your vaults, and the purple was delicious.

The two of you perform this gracious dance every morning, regardless of what else is happening on your globe. You say: 'I'll move like this, and you move like that.' Brother Sun says: 'I'll bathe you in light, and then soothe you with dark.' You say: 'Can we keep dancing?' Brother Sun smiles and says: 'For a very very very long time.'

Watching you both reminded me of the enormity of everything. What's a sleepless night? Watching you reassured me of your reliability. Watching you gave me a little fizz of pleasure at the beauty that blesses us.

I did feel a teensy bit jealous of Aiko as she lazed in her cosy bed this morning. She only deigned to raise her head for a corner of toast, so I could check that she was feeling a bit better.

I'm glad she's feeling better. And I'm feeling better too – being tired feels okay now. Maybe I'll be grumpy later, maybe I'll nap, maybe not. Tonight Brother Sun will slide away from view and I can go to sleep smiling at your dance.

Love, Satya

Dear Earth, we are not alone

This weekend eighteen Buddhists from different traditions came together in your name, dear Earth. We are all members of Extinction Rebellion and we wanted to feel less alone.

At the start of the first day I led an exercise where we all stand in a circle facing each other. Someone calls out a category which they themselves belong to – 'who's got a dog?' or 'who's vegan?'. Everyone who belongs to that category then steps forwards into the middle, and we look around at each other in recognition.

We called out many categories – who likes cycling, who's not heterosexual, who has a sibling who's died – and mostly we were not alone. This not-being-met happened just twice – only one of us liked engines, and I can't remember the second one. Of course if the circle was bigger they wouldn't have been alone.

It made everyone happy. It's good to remember the things we have in common – we spend so long focusing on our differences. When I feel nervous about speaking in front of an audience, it helps me to remember that the people in front of me also all drink and pee and sleep and cry. We are all made of the same messy stuff. We all want to be loved.

We are not alone, darling Earth. Whatever we feel, somebody somewhere will get it. We have each other, we have you, and we have your marvelously abundant flora and fauna.

Who was born to a mother? Who is going to die? Who

gets afraid sometimes in the night? Who has a heart that pumps? Who yearns? Who breathes?

Love, Satya

Dear Earth, I am not in control of the universe

"Whenever I've got a problem, whenever I'm in pain, whenever I'm unhappy, I have to at least be open to the possibility that the reason for it is that I think I'm in control of the universe. It's often that." ~ Russell Brand

Over the past few weeks, dear Earth, I've been allowing myself to be guided. I've remembered that my own ideas about what I should and shouldn't be doing are at best limited, and are at worst are driven by greed, small-mindedness and fear.

I've been shown repeatedly in my life that if I can step out of the way, I am taken in a 'Good Orderly Direction'. Things that seemed terrible at the time turned out to be exactly what I needed, and things I was desperate for and grabbed at turned out to be not at all what I hoped they'd be.

What does 'stepping out of the way' actually look like? It means that instead of tuning out the boring person in the meeting, I remain curious about what they have to say. It means that I say yes to the unexpected invitation and see where it takes me. It means that I wait, watch and wonder. It means that I stop trying to control the universe.

I am not proposing a kind of avoidant quietism. When I allow myself to be guided I am often called to act, and this can involve doing things that take some courage.

I am saying that when I listen to something bigger-than-me, dear Earth, it helps. Sometimes this is you. Sometimes it is the Buddha. Sometimes it is the boring person in the meeting. When I keep my ears open and put my own ideas on hold, what happens is always more wonderful than my best laid plans.

I spend a lot of my time trying to be in control. It frightens me and it frustrates me and it tires me out. Today didn't go to plan. I didn't do the work I was hoping to, and I didn't handle the distractions very gracefully. My printer wouldn't behave. I frittered an hour of the afternoon away on Twitter. I hated it.

When I stopped hating it, I realised that the world hadn't ended, and that I had learned some things about myself. When I stop trying to swim in straight lines and bob along with the eddies and the swirls, the view is more beautiful, I get where I need to go faster, and I can lie back and enjoy the awesome ride.

Much love, Satya

Dear Earth, this is for you

At the end of our Buddhist services we often transfer merit. This means that we symbolically gather together all the peace, insight, consolation and joy that we've received from our practice together, and we pass it on to those who might need it.

The great thing about transferring merit is that, in the giving, we receive. I am glad when I think of those who might be standing under a shower of our blessings. Maybe you absorb some our happiness, dear Earth, or maybe someone walking past the temple suddenly glimpses a single beam of light where before there was none.

Giving isn't always this easy. When it comes to my freshly baked peanut butter brownies, my generosity increases or decreases depending on how many brownies there are and how many people are present. A full tin of brownies and a few people – my generosity knows no bounds. When the brownies are running low…

This is how it is for all of us. Those of us who aren't enlightened just yet, anyway. Sometimes we are able to offer freely, but mostly our clinging-at-things gets in the way. We cling because we are afraid of scarcity, or of facing unsavoury truths about ourselves or the world. It is human to cling, and pointless to pretend that it is otherwise.

When I do find myself having a generous thought, when I experience the pure joy of giving, this is a cause for celebration. When we give things in this spirit it's just like transferring merit – our happiness increases. At these times I see that I am only passing on what I have already been given.

In our liturgy it says "Gratitude is multiplying, going forth, returning richly..." Here is my happiness from this morning, dear reader, dear Earth. Please, take it. It would be my pleasure.

Much love, Satya

Dear Earth, in praise of wet afternoons

In praise of finds on the wet forest floor: a snapped off squirm of pale root imitating a worm, a majestically spiked conker coat, a lime strip of moss like the sloughed-off pelt of a mini beast.

In praise of the chance meeting of three dogs on the hill, strangers for a few seconds only, who delight in each other's smells and exuberance, chasing each other away and back in a dance of Right Now.

In praise of the invention of wellingtons and waterproof trousers, and of purple socks that keep my toes toasty, and of a hoodless rain-kissed head so I can be closer to you, darling Earth.

Harder, granted, to praise little dogs who don't like being in selfies, and then dash away when you try to put them back on the lead. Despite the offer of juicy sweet-potato treats, despite the feigning of disinterest, despite stern words.

Still. Then there is a warm shower to ease clots of mud from fur. Then there is steaming redbush tea in a favourite mug. And now there is this blackbird, dueting with Carrie Cleveland as she sings about love in 1978.

This blackbird is going to break my heart, sweet Earth.

With gratitude that goes on and on, Satya

Dear Earth, a confession of unfaithfulness

Sweet Earth, this is a confession. As I write these love letters to you, I am being unfaithful. A part of me is devoted to you, and another part is greedy for the praise that I will receive for what I write.

I can feel kindly towards this greedy part. It is trying to receive love in the only way it knows – through performing, through manipulating, through flattery. It believes that, if I stop putting my writing into the world, I will be instantly forgotten. It believes that I am only as valuable as my last book. It believes that love depends on usefulness.

I would like to learn from your common primroses, lovely Earth. They grow in shady corners, pastel yellow with yolky splashes at their centres. They don't agitate their leaves or crane their blossoms to seek attention. Sometimes their ordinary beauty is noticed, and sometimes it isn't – it's all the same to them. They soak up the sun and feel the water running up through their xylem. Is it foolish to imagine that they are happy?

When the praise-greedy part settles down, dear Earth, I am happy. I linger over describing your dangling catkins, your flint walls, your hazy blue horizon. I enjoy the taste of words as I roll them around in my mouth. I know that everything I have is yours, borrowed.

Dear Earth, let me be a primrose.

Love, Satya

Dear Earth, will you be my friend?

We have a friend who moves slowly and who is an introverted deep-thinker. He had a beautiful mellow Labrador companion for many years. When our little dog Aiko introduced herself to him when she was a puppy she raced around him, jumping up inappropriately, running away and then back, trying to get him to chase her.

He confessed to us that he didn't know what to do with her. There was no meeting point between them – no way of entering into relationship. It reminded me of Aiko's 'friendship' with our cats, who she loves, but who hiss and swipe at her constantly as she gets right up in their face and then attaches her nose to their bottoms and follows them around.

Recently, after many months, Aiko and our friend have begun to make each other's acquaintance. It began with a stick which was thrown and retrieved, thrown and retrieved. When Aiko is racing back towards you with a stick in her mouth, it is difficult not to be infected by her massive grin.

Sometimes it's hard to make friends, dear Earth, with your strange humans, your animals, your objects and your landscapes. Sometimes the other is oblivious or hostile. Sometimes we're trying to make friends with each other, but we're just not speaking the same language.

What helps? Time. Curiosity. Playfulness. Faith in the goodness hiding in others. An open mind. An awareness of our own sore spots and what pokes at them. A willingness to learn a different language. Forgiveness. A big happy grin.

Last week our friend created a special pile of sticks in the garden, just for Aiko. Yesterday he looked at her with astonishment and exclaimed, 'hasn't she got beautiful eyes?'

Help me to find the beauty in everything and everyone, darling Earth. Help me to make friends with all of you.

Love, Satya

Dear Earth, help me to take pauses

"Build gaps in your life. Pauses. Proper pauses."
~ Thom Yorke

My husband Kaspa is away and so I am in charge of the temple. Mornings consist of cleaning litter trays (and all the other places our old cat has deemed equivalent), getting the bunnies up, giving medication, searching for dog poo in the garden, and all the other tasks that are necessary when you somehow end up with seven pets.

This morning I heard my blue bench whisper to me on the way back to the flat. "Satya! You haven't sat on me for ages!" And so I did. For ten minutes I sat with a little dog on my lap and looked out across the valley. Strong winds were shoving heavy clouds across the ceiling of the sky. Splodges of early Spring colour had arrived: a bush with candy-pink flowers, deep purple primroses, even a baby daffodil. The sun was hidden and leaking rays. I rose grateful, and changed.

On some days, even a few minutes of space feels impossible. How could we stop doing, when there is so much to be done? If we stopped, what might we feel?

You know about pauses, wise Earth. Your bulbs, your bears, your trees – they all have a good long sleep once a year. Your African daisies close at night to preserve their pollen. Our human bodies are built on pauses: our liver works more slowly at night, we relax in the space between each breath, we take a tenth of a second rest with every blink.

Dear Earth, when we gobble our days, we neglect to taste them. We get indigestion. It makes sense that we rush.

The sickness in our society encourages it. We also have many complex systems inside us that are protecting us from our own depths, where they fear that monsters are waiting. Pauses sometimes do allow old parts of us to rise up from our subconscious, but they are never monsters. However scary they look they are always alone, afraid, and in need of love.

Pauses are the salt and pepper of our days. They are the cat on your lap, purr-engine running. They are sitting in the dark after the credits of a dazzling film.

Dear Earth, help me to take pauses. Help me to taste each and every mouthful of your feast.

Much love, Satya

Dear Earth, we are so vulnerable

The coronavirus is killing our comrades. 6.7 million people in Yemen are relying on food aid. A few days ago, a twenty five year old colleague died suddenly. He had been working full time with those who want to save you, dear Earth.

Outside, a few flakes of wet snow are diving past the hazel catkins and the dark ivy and nestling into the grass. I look away, write a sentence, and when I look back the snow has stopped and the sun is blazing.

The weather changes. Viruses blow in and out again. War blooms and rots. Some of us will die as we expect to die, from the third cancer at an advanced age, and some of us will be taken much sooner. What can we do?

Yesterday two women came to clean the temple, as an offering. Kaspa paused for ten minutes this morning to fuss our old cat. This afternoon we ate chocolate cake with our friend, who has been alive for exactly fifty four years. The magnolia tree is budding.

We can love each other while we are here. We can be kind to everything that is cowering or lashing out. We can praise your magnificence, darling Earth. When we need to, we can lean into your soft chest and rest.

Love Satya

Dear Earth, you are burning and I am small

If I returned home to a fire in my living room, I would hurtle to the fire extinguisher. If my dog was slicked in dark oil, I would wash her gently, carefully and thoroughly. If my little nieces were starving, I would steal to feed them.

Dear Earth, you are burning. You are melting, and choking, and being poisoned. Your children are dying. Your animals are being wiped out. I am so small. I am so selfish, and limited, and weak. Where do I begin? How can I rest when you are in such pain? How can I bear it?

When I am aching with the pain of the world and despairing at the insufficiency of my response, I remember what Jesus said. He promised that his yoke is light. He promised that, if we follow a spiritual path, we won't be asked to carry more than we are able to carry.

What stops me from going crazy in these crazy times is asking the Buddha (my Higher Power, the Universe, God, you) to tell me what to do next. If I left it to the various parts of me, I would flip between manic activity and numb denial, overwhelm and torpor. I would spend all my rest days soaked in guilt. I would judge everything I did as not-enough, pathetic, cowardly, or lazy. I would burn out or retreat into comforting fantasy.

Mostly, sweet Earth, you tell me to do very ordinary things. Listen properly to that person's fears. Write this. Give the cat his medicine. Go to that boring meeting. Pull weeds from the vegetable patch. Sometimes you tell me to get arrested, or to speak up when I'm afraid to. Nothing you've asked of me has been too much. You often say the word 'gentle' to me. You often remind me to rest.

Will we put out enough fires in time to save you or, more accurately, to save ourselves? I don't know. Some days I am pregnant with hope for our future. Some days, I think it's more realistic to accept that the human race has entered their end-time. And if the tipping points are already behind us? I still want to do what I can while I can.

Dear Earth, please show me what to use my limited energy on today. Please forgive me for the paltriness of my efforts in the face of your great suffering. Please help me remember that your yoke is light, and that you want me to be happy, and to know myself as beloved.

Bowing before you with gratitude, beautiful Earth.

Love, Satya

Dear Earth, you are lush

Your lushness is infinite, but today I want to single out this soup. The clear, happy orange of fresh carrots. The velvet richness of roasted squash. An electric hint of ginger. A splash of lemon. Salt.

For years I ordered a weekly veg box from a large company. I liked that I could say what vegetables I did want, and which I didn't. I was fussy, and quick to complain if a vegetable was spoiled, or if there wasn't enough variety.

Now we order our veg from our local farm, and the growing is done by Rachel and her small team. When the box arrives, it's a gift. Look what she's grown! Even at this time of year – long beets, tender baby rainbow chard, a huge knobbly celeriac, a glossy red cabbage...

There's no asking for certain veg, or banning others. What arrives is what the field is offering. Week after week, I exchange a paltry amount of cash for all Rachel's work, all that weather, all those nutrients, all that amazing flavour.

Darling Earth, your squash and carrot soup has nourished my body and my spirit. Allow me to offer these words to you, and my gratitude, which is overflowing.

Love, Satya

Dear Earth, eco-living is a pain

Yesterday at 5pm I was sitting in a very cold train station, at the end of a very long day, with two changes and an hour and a half of travelling ahead of me. If I'd taken my car instead I'd have been home and cosy ten minutes ago. Phooey.

Making ecological choices often involves some inconvenience. I've given up flying and so holidays abroad are mostly out. I spend a small fortune on eco-dog food, peat-free compost and deodorant in cardboard tubes. I feel awkward mentioning climate change when talking with strangers about the extreme weather, as I make a point of doing.

Of course, as a middle class white woman living in the Global North, being able to focus on these choices is a huge privilege. I'm not worried about whether this year's crops will feed my children, or whether I'm going to have my freedoms curtailed by an oppressive regime.

It's good to remember this, and it's also good to be realistic, and to start where we are. For many of us, enjoying the taste of meat or butter gets in the way of us committing to a plant-based diet. An over-full life means we don't have time to walk instead of driving. Needing to feel 'normal' or to fit in at the office makes it hard to choose second hand clothes. If that's where we are, that's where we are. We can notice this resistance when it arises, and meet it with friendly understanding. We can acknowledge the fears underneath.

I found a waiting room at the train station. It was warm, and it even smelt good! I read about a drug addict in

Japan who was in recovery, and her story lit up my evening. Maybe it was okay to be where I was after all.

When we are in the right frame of mind, the 'pain' of eco-living becomes a joy. We cherish the slow walk to the bakery. We enjoy getting to know our own country on holidays. We relish the delicious sweetness of our locally grown organic parsnips.

We reconnect with gratitude, and suddenly we are the recipients of endless abundance.

Thank you, dear Earth.

Love, Satya

Dear Earth, life is closer than death

On Tuesday evening we heard our cat Tsuki suddenly wailing in the corridor. By the time I reached her, her soul had slipped quietly out of her body.

"Mara follows every step." We recite this Buddhist text every morning, and it reminds us that death and destruction is always closer than we can imagine. Tsuki was only eight years old, and before her sudden death she was apparently healthy. She was enjoying her usual activities – happily dribbling on my lap while I typed at this computer, watching the world from the blue bench outside, crawling into the cosy caves made by our duvet at night.

Darling Earth, I don't have to tell you about death. Death offers us building materials for the next generation. Without death, there would be no room for fresh life. Death intensifies creativity, joy, energy, passion and compassion.

Sometimes we can ward death off for a good while. We dose our twenty year old cat with various medications every day – without them he'd have left us four years ago.

Us humans had a natural life-span at home on you too, dear Earth, before you became inhospitable to us. It was a very very very long time. We've messed that up. We've smoked too much carbon and eaten too many rainforests and excreted too much plastic.

We might be able to save the human race, and we might not. Either way, we can offer you medicine and begin to heal you. We can plant trees and stop runways being built and rise up against the companies doing the most horrific damage. We can keep our eyes open to the truth, and share it. We can sit outside Parliament and pray through the cold nights. We can come together. We can act.

We can also remember to enjoy soft warm purring cats while they are here. We can linger with shy aubergine-coloured hellebores and brassy daffodils. We can savour the taste of cherry chocolate, and breathe in the fragrant steam rising from our cup of tea.

Death is close, and life is closer.

Love, Satya

Dear Earth, who are you?

Yesterday I was filmed for a Dutch programme about Extinction Rebellion. One of the questions Wouter asked me was, "Who are you writing to?" It's an interesting question. Are you a figment of my imagination, sweet Earth? Am I talking to myself?

My vague answer to him (a deity, a living organism, infinite complexity and compassion) didn't quite satisfy me. I was clear about my answer to the next question, though. "Does she talk back to you?" Yes. Yes, you do.

You are talking to me right now, as I rest my ceramic mug on my cupped palm and delicious heat soaks into my cold fingertips. You speak to me as you riffle the long tassels of catkins outside my window, showing me how to stay flexible. The precision of this goldfinch delicately taking a sunflower heart is a reminder that we are all beloved. Frogspawn crowding our pond whispers 'abundance' and 'miracles'.

Who are you, dear Earth? Who am I writing to? I have no idea. I feel the same way when I talk to the Buddha, or to God.

What I do know is that writing to you helps me to make sense of things. It helps me to snuggle in closer to your silky grasses and to your cool streams. It gives me faith when I am trembling, and balm when I am ragged. It helps me to listen for directions, instructions and solutions. It reminds me to *enjoy* you.

It helps me to love you, and to trust that I am loved.

Love, Satya

Dear Earth, I sat up all night for you

I arrived at midday and sat down on the pavement outside Parliament. It was cold. Rain bucketed down on us, soaking my coat and the cushion I was going to sit on. We put away the extinguished candles. We rearranged the wet signs, which let passers-by know that we were holding a vigil for you, precious Earth.

My friend Sarah and I joyfully chanted for you as raindrops hit our cheeks: Om Ami Dewa Hri. I met Fazeela and walked to Downing Street where I stood in solidarity with a lot of Muslim women I didn't know as they spoke of Kashmir, Gaza, Yemen. Later we sat in a circle on the drying pavement and Yael led her Jewish colleagues, us Buddhists, and the Christians, in a lesson about the fast of Esther, and we all sang a Jewish song with great gusto.

The night shift arrived – Joe and Yogaratna. We turned the hourglass and sat silently for half hour after half hour as the sand ran out. Joe rang the bells and we bowed. I drifted off for five minutes, ten, ensconced in my purple plastic mac, with seven layers of clothes just about keeping the chill from my bones. We walked across Westminster bridge to the hospital cafe for hot tea at 3am.

I chanted for you, dear Earth. Hours of chanting and meditating and praying. I offered my tiny voice to the vast sky as the commuters streamed past us on Monday morning, thousands of them, most of them not turning to glance at us.

In the afternoon a woman with beautiful wrinkles approached us with tears streaming down her face. She said, 'I am with you.' She gave her gloves to Sarah, whose fingers were freezing. She allowed the gratitude and the grief to pour out of her. She clasped my hands tight and held on and, as I type, the tears come to me again.

It was a small thing, a small thing, to sit up all night for you, darling Earth. Around the globe, people are dying in your name.

It was a privilege to lean against the cold wall that surrounds our government, and to watch the trees in the park catch stars in their branches. It was a privilege to beam compassion out around me, smiling whenever anyone's eyes settled on me. It was a privilege to hold you in my heart, sweet Earth, as the virus swirls, as the forests burn, as your water becomes bitter with our poisons.

The morning light blushed through the darkness. Another day. We have another shining day.

With so much gratitude, Satya

Dear Earth, why pray?

Here is a photo of me and my friend Sarah from our vigil for you, sweet Earth, that continued all day and all night for weeks until the virus forced us back into our homes. I can't remember who had just told a joke, but I love the smile playing on Sarah's lips.

We spent a lot of time sitting and doing nothing for you, dear Earth. We could have been running for our local council, or writing angry letters, or planting forests.

We sat with our signs – Jews, Muslims, secular meditators, lawyers, travellers, grandmothers – freezing cold, elated, and despairing. We watched thousands of eyes swerving away from us as office workers walked their brisk walk to work. Some people nodded their thanks at us, signaling their agreement. A few people spat hate at us with their looks or with their words.

Why pray for you, dear Earth? Why sit on the streets and let grief swish around in our bodies? Why waste our time beaming love at you when we could be doing something?

Because I know that you are witnessing us, as we ourselves bear witness. This is my small contribution to the bouquet of actions you need, and I know that it matters. I know that love placed into the Universe is never lost, but finds its way slowly to where it is needed, as inexorably as water.

Love Satya

Dear Earth, let's be kind to each other

A new virus has made itself at home inside us, darling Earth. It is creating heavy work for us – emotional, practical, financial, political. It is killing those who are the most vulnerable. Many of us are frightened.

When we are frightened, we do what our systems know how to do. For some of us, that means hiding under a fleecy blanket of denial – scoffing at the doomsayers, sure of our own indestructibility. For others, that means mobilising into hypervigilence and panic – checking the news at ten minute intervals, hoarding pasta, our thoughts circling horribly.

We are frail beings, and we want to live. When there is a direct threat to our existence, we move mountains. This selfishness is programmed in, and it manifests in many different ways.

We can be kind to the parts of us that are trying to protect us. If our system becomes overwhelmed, we're no use to anyone. Our managing parts, our distancers, our compulsions, all of them are trying to steady the ship.

We can be kind to the parts of other people that are trying to protect them – by obsessing, by discounting us and our experience, by shutting us down. When we can't see any kindness in them, we can trust that they're doing the best they can with the resources they have.

Our leaders will make mistakes. They'll be slow, and they'll prioritise in ways we disagree with. Our friends may infuriate us. We'll find ourselves obsessing over tiny details, or being upset by things we feel we 'shouldn't' feel upset about.

It's all understandable. We can keep listening to the parts of us that are afraid, and be patient with them as we would be with a tired child. We can try to understand their motivations, and appreciate how hard they are working for us, even as they're causing chaos. As we do this, we may find compassion welling up – finding a way past the layers and layers of protection, like sweet nectar.

We can remember, then, that we are not alone. We can offer help where it is needed – a phone-call, a delivery of groceries. We can find the steady ground underneath us, regardless of what happens next. We can lean into your soft green lap, lovely Earth. We can radiate gentleness.

Brother Sun is still lighting up the blades of grass in the garden. Each of them is reaching up towards him, with longing and in thanks.

Let us be very kind to each other, those of us who are alive this sparkling day.

With much love, Satya

Dear Earth, today I was a hot mess

I didn't get out of my pyjamas. I snapped at my husband. I ate far too much pasta and vegan parmesan for dinner. I watched documentaries about abuse on Netflix. I checked for fresh news of the virus every six minutes or so.

Oh Earth, I am such a human human. I've been prodding at my selfishness like a sore gum – am I social distancing because I want to protect vulnerable others, or because I'm afraid for myself? Am I gobbling news to become better informed, or because it gives me a weird adrenaline high? Why aren't I one of the good people who are checking on their elderly neighbours? When should I start properly hoarding high quality chocolate?

I feel better than I did. What helped? Time. Going to a twelve step meeting and hearing from other humans about their own aching vulnerabilities. Remembering how much sicker it makes me when I get sucked in online. Chasing my little dog around the flat at high speed, and being chased back.

More than anything, it helped me to remember that we are in an unprecedented global situation, and that I should maybe cut myself a little slack. It's hard enough to be an ordinary human some days, never mind during a pandemic. I looked at myself in the mirror, called myself a hot mess, and smiled.

Thanks for listening, dear Earth.

Love, Satya

Dear Earth, everything is changing

I look at the blank page for a long time.

What can I say? What can I possibly say that will even begin to make sense of it all? That will provide some comfort?

The boiler in the room next to me is thrumming. It is heating this whole house – keeping us warm like a fleece-lined jacket with deep pockets and a hood.

Outside a single blackbird is doodling on the silence with his liquid notes. They slide up and down, slippery, exact, pure.

Start where you are. What can you hear? What is supporting your body? What can your eyes rest on?

Everything is changing. And, you are holding me, sweet Earth. You are feeding me. You are filling my lungs with plant-breath. You are offering me posies of pale yellow cowslips, and a pond brimming with squirming tadpoles just out of their squishy spawn.

On the hills yesterday I met a deaf man and his huge black dog Kuma, which means bear in Japanese. Little Aiko and him sniffed each other's smells as we tried to understand each other. We connected over trivialities for a few minutes, and warmth grew between us. We parted ways. I cupped the little glow close.

Can you feel the beginnings of this warmth? It comes whenever we remember that everything is changing, and that everything is sacred. Huge happy dogs, delicate cowslips, our old cat's bony chest as it heaves.

There will be fear. There will be grief. If it is here right now, invite it in. Offer it a cup of tea. Show it the ground underneath you. Brush its cheek, softly, softly, as you would an over-tired child. Allow your breath to be lullabies.

Dear Earth, everything is changing. What will help? This. Tell me what you see, and let it love you.

Love, Satya

Dear Earth, I have been fretting about death

We are in the fists of a pandemic, and fretting about death has preoccupied me. I have been resisting the fact of my almost total lack of control. I have been reassuring myself with lies about my invulnerability. I have been checking for new news every ten minutes and pulling at the fear like a hangnail.

Meanwhile, sparks of electric blue are budding on the green alkanet, and the pond is full of squirming black commas.

I have been neglecting you, darling Earth. Like a bear with a sore paw, I have been nursing my small pains and closing my eyes to yours. You are still running a temperature. You are still having your blood poisoned and your feathery green fur ripped out. You are still watching us as we fail to save sixteen thousand children, the ones who will die today (and tomorrow, and tomorrow) because they don't have enough to eat.

I have been nursing my small fears, which are terrifyingly big when they loom so close, and this is understandable, and appropriate, and forgivable.

Yesterday I tucked sleeping vegetable seeds into dark pots. Soon they will stir, stretch, and reach up for Brother Sun.

When I think of the magic inside seeds, I am not so afraid of dying. When I watch my bunnies grooming each other, when I listen to a lonely stranger, when I plunge my hands into hot washing up water, I am not so afraid of dying.

Dying will come. When fear arises, I will tend to it. When a pumpkin seed sprouts, I will water it. When joy floats up like a wren's song, I will embrace it.

Dear Earth, help me to remember these small tasks, the things I can do today. Help me to remember the comforts of impermanence. Help me to remember your wide lap, where I can rest. Help me to keep loving you.

Love, Satya

Dear Earth, I am not worthy

Other people are fitting ventilators to those suffering in the overflowing hospitals, dear Earth. Other people are fetching medicine for their neighbours. I sit sulking in my home office and wait for my allowed daily exercise. I order myself expensive chocolates and a green hourglass. I estimate the days until I am free from this extravagant jail.

The part of me that feels worthless is here. She is very young. She was shown that she needed to work hard if she wanted attention. She came to believe that there was something very wrong with her.

It doesn't help this part when I tell her that she's just got it all wrong. Rohr says, "From the beginning, receiving God's love has never been a 'worthiness contest'. This is very hard for almost everyone to accept." She feels so terrible that other parts of me panic and work feverishly to cover up her feelings. These busy parts drove me to write nine books and to build a full psychotherapy practice. They pushed me to run this temple and to grow a big congregation. It is never enough to stop the worthlessness from leaking out.

The young part doesn't want to hear that she's got it wrong. She just wants to be held. She wants to hear that it makes sense that she feels worthless – anyone in her position would. She wants me to show her that I taste the flavours of her pain and of her loneliness.

She sees my tears for her, and it soothes her. Now I can look up and see how much weight we are all carrying, in these strange new times. I can see how coronavirus is holding a magnifying glass to our courage and our generosity, as well as to our selfishness, our paranoia, and our myriad fears. I can see how hard I'm working, even when it doesn't look like it from the outside. I can see that I am enough.

The love begins to seep into me, like water into the chard and beetroot seeds I've just sown in the vegetable patch. Green shoots will come. For now, I'm going to wait quietly in the dark.

With tender love for you and for all, Satya

Dear Earth, this is making me happy

I am looking at the rectangle of land in front of our flat, generously dressed in dark compost.

Most of it is mushroom compost, which arrived on a lorry. The man asked me to get my own pen to sign for it as he wasn't allowed to lend me his or I might infect him with the virus. Some of it is bunny compost, made from our three bunnies' poo and urine-soaked straw and newspaper, fermented in our four black dalek composters. One of them had become home to three fat rats, and I squealed as they skittered to safety.

Why am I so happy, dear Earth? Like all happinesses, it has mixed provenance. Some comes from a release of tension. This compost cushions me from the fear of not having enough to eat. It represents the small control I do have, in a world that has recently shown me empty supermarket shelves. It also satisfies the parts of me that push me to Do More Stuff, and looking at it reminds them of my hard labour.

These happinesses are valid, and appropriate. I will enjoy them.

There is also the joy that comes from grace. Gratitude for the abundance of this nutrient-rich stuff, more than we've ever managed to gift our veg patch before. Excitement about the coming weeks, as chard and lettuce seeds will start sprouting and as the Turk's Turban squashes and all the others emerge in our window sill pots. Anticipation of the deliciousness of food grown metres away from our front door. Appreciation of the extra time we'll have at weekends to tend it, now we're in lockdown.

There will be troubles. I predict slugs, white fly on the kale, wild bunny nibbling and dud seeds. There will be more. This is the deal with life – we do what we can, and we hand the rest over. For two years in a row now I have abandoned my dream of blackcurrant jam, as the birds have gorged on the lot when I wasn't looking.

And, today I am happy. In return, I promise to water the baby courgette plants. I promise to stake the beans and put anti-slug sheep's wool around their ankles. I promise to sow tender care with the seeds, and to say thank you for everything I harvest – to this compost, to Brother Sun, to the miracle-maker.

I promise to relish every drop of goodness that comes my way. It is my happy duty.

Thank you, dear Earth.

Love, Satya

Dear Earth, it's impossible

All year I have been avoiding plastic in the supermarkets. Last week I chose the mushrooms sweating in a cling-filmed plastic coffin, because I was afraid. I was afraid of catching the coughing virus.

Meanwhile, on a Pacific island, albatross chicks are being fed lighters, bottle tops, and biros by their mothers. This cargo fills their stomachs and stops them from lifting off, and so they die where they were born. Their soft bodies melt back into the ground and they leave behind a mound of our plastic shame.

Dear Earth, human beings are suffering right now across the globe. How can we ask the man who isn't allowed to visit his dying grandfather in hospital to think about your coral reefs? How can we expect the struggling single mother to worry about rainforests? How can we get frightened citizens to challenge their government on the climate crisis as the pandemic spreads?

It's impossible, darling Earth. As I write this letter to you, I look outside at the lime-green leaves budding on the silver birch and tears graze the back of my throat. It is grief for the albatross chick, for the grandfather, and for the mother. As I feel it, I am held by your beauty and your resilience and your infinite complexity. I see how you make space for the delicacy of peonies and swifts nests, the resilience of granite, the persistence of water. I see that your tender care is always bigger than the suffering you witness.

We will emerge from this acute crisis, with many dead and with much rebuilding to do. Will we use what we have learnt? Will we harness the same courage and decisiveness to tackle the much bigger crisis that continues to unfold, the one that looms like an elephant over a mouse?

Dear Earth, it's impossible. And. You can help us to grow our hearts, and when there's room for grief, there is always room for green shoots.

With much love, Satya

Dear Earth, change is slower than we'd like

Before getting our first dog, I asked everyone I met about dog-cat relationships. How would our cats cope with a new puppy? What could we do to make it easier for them? I bought a huge cat tree for them to retreat into, I read up on all the training techniques, and our ball of puppy-fluff finally arrived.

Aiko loved the cats. She loved it most when she hurled herself at them and they sprinted away. I tried to keep her on a lead when they were around, but it only took a couple of top-speed circuits around the garden and she was hooked.

Despite our best efforts, relations remained cool. The cats never came down from the cat tree, and I felt like a failure. One of our young cats Tsuki died unexpectedly, followed a few weeks later by our old man cat. Roshi remained – the cat who'd always been the most frightened of Aiko. I resigned myself to a decade of keeping them separated.

After a whole year of being afraid, Roshi started holding his ground on the living room carpet as Aiko sniffed him enthusiastically. A week later he was relaxed enough to roll belly-up in the sun with Aiko lying just next to him. Yesterday he sniffed Aiko's face and then head-butted the air in front of her – it may just have been a mistake, but I'm taking it as the beginnings of affection.

Sometimes change is fast, and sometimes it's slow. Sometimes we have trust that roots are making their way deep underground, out of sight. We can learn to wait, as Isak Dineson advised, 'without hope, without despair'.

You know about this, dear Earth. You know about the formation of glaciers and the slow flourishing of moss. You trust that tadpoles will become frogs in their own time. We are the ones who carry clocks with us. We are the ones who throw money at the things we want to go faster. How arrogant we are, and how we set ourselves up for disappointment.

I will welcome my impatient and frustrated parts, great Earth, and notice my elaborate attempts at manipulation. These bits of me are all trying to help me feel better – I get it. I'll make space for them all, and send them all compassion. As they settle, I'm left with clarity about what I can do, and what I need to hand over. I'm left with spaciousness. From that place, I'll witness the beautiful terrible astonishing unfurling of the future. Who knows what will come next?

Love, Satya

Dear Earth, I believe in miracles

Oh Earth, we are suffering. The virus is amongst us. We are seeing how it is to run out of food and to be afraid of going out. We shiver as death blows in at our perimeters. We are tasting our powerlessness. When this is over, what will we do?

Will we dive back into consumption, compulsion, control? Will we book tickets for far-away holidays, get back on the roads, prop up our economy, go back to undervaluing those who do our dirty work, pick up where we left off? If not, who is going to give up half of everything they have? Who is going to willingly hand over their security? Who is going to let go of their old comforts? Are they? Am I?

I believe in miracles, darling Earth, because I have seen them. I have met walking miracles in the rooms of Alcoholic Anonymous across the world. I have seen the brittle carapaces of my psychotherapy clients melted by the Universe's care. I have seen hummingbird hawk moths, forgiveness, a volcano, seeds sprouting, sudden peace, newborn babies.

It will take many miracles to save our species, sweet Earth. The veins of our greed, hate and delusion run very deep. It is natural that we would want to cling on to safety. You see that, and you forgive us.

Underneath all the panic, the violence and the avoidance of shame is something even more powerful. This is the meat of miracles. It is dogged, radical, tender, loyal, astonishingly beautiful.

It has been gently raining all night, after weeks of dry weather which has baked the earth. Each drop is confirmation of what is possible.

Love from Satya

Dear Earth, what can I see?

I can see our vegetable patch through my office window. There are our month-old seedlings – courgettes, kale, cauliflower, cucumber, squash. Ruffled green sprigs of potato leaves have poked their way up through the earth. There is flimsy lettuce, just-germinated chard, and a self-seeded marigold which has been socking us in the eye with luminous orange flowers for weeks.

A few nights ago you sent us some heavy weather, dear Earth. The wind howled, and I sat inside worrying for our seedlings. In the morning one courgette plant was snapped in two, and that was all. It seemed miraculous.

We are all weathering some heavy weather right now. Across the globe, a virus is snapping people in half. The collateral damage is massive and we are still at the beginning. As usual, those who are already vulnerable will suffer more. Our friends who have lived a long time. Our friends whose bodies are already weak. Our friends in refugee camps, in prisons, in countries with weak healthcare systems, in villages where there isn't enough to eat.

We are getting an early taste of how it will be when your systems break down, darling Earth. When the thick blanket of carbon dioxide raises your temperature by just two degrees more. When extreme weather gets more extreme, and more lethal. When we begin to forget all the species we have lost. When empty supermarket shelves become the new normal. When we can no longer keep our children safe.

How is it possible to face this great suffering? How is it possible to live with our fear, our grief, our rage, our hopelessness, without it overwhelming us? How can we prepare for the heavy dark clouds on the horizon?

My grey stone Buddha sits on my windowsill, just where I can see him. He knows all about the foolishness of the human race, and he doesn't despair of us. He holds stillness in his body as if it were a flower. He watches it all unfold and his compassion is unbroken.

Don't forget to water your seedlings, he says to me. The bird seed needs topping up – look, a goldfinch is waiting. When you go through to make yourself a cup of tea, don't forget to pause and stroke your dogs. Ralph is dreaming, maybe of rabbits, and little squeaks escape him as his legs judder. As he feels my hand on his flanks he sighs, stretches, and settles.

Sometimes the storms will break those around us, or leave us with wounds that never heal. When this happens, the Buddha is there to console us. Sometimes seedlings survive storms, and the whipping wind strengthens their stems, and they grow stronger than before. When this happens, the Buddha is there to encourage us. Sometimes storms bring new seeds, and astonishingly beautiful new life. When this happens, the Buddha is there to celebrate with us.

There will be tragedies, and there will be miracles, precious Earth. Right now, a pigeon is waddling between the vegetable plants, finding tasty things to eat. The white splash around his neck and the blush at his chest are quite wonderful.

Love, Satya

Dear Earth, relationship is complicated

Ralph the seven month old Shih Tzu came to live with us a fortnight ago. Our dog Aiko always loves to meet other dogs when we're out walking, and I hadn't quite appreciated how it might be for her to have a new sibling.

A little brother who snatches her toys from her mouth. Who runs to meet and greet us first. Who follows her everywhere. Who eats the breakfast she was leaving for later. Who has the audacity to jump up onto *her green chair*.

Life is full of knots and tangles. One way of making things less complicated is to separate ourselves off. I see myself doing this all the time. I distract myself from the suffering of other people. I shove the hurting parts of myself into cupboards. I blunt the grief and fear I feel about your predicament, darling Earth.

Aiko and Ralph have been involved in negotiations all fortnight. There has been a lot of play wrestling, protracted discussion about how best to share the antler, and some pretty stern rebuking. It's a lot to adjust to, and they each have their peccadilloes (as do we all). Things are settling. The growl-warnings are few and far between. They run happy rings around each other in the garden, explore on walks two-abreast, lie close to each other. This morning Ralph napped with his head on Aiko's stomach.

Dear Earth, help me to come into closer relationship with all of you. Help me to weather the storming. Help me remember that intimacy takes us through discomfort and into an open, sunny field.

Love, Satya

Dear Earth, I'm leaning in

I'm resting my foot against a warm snoring dog underneath my desk.

I'm resting my eyes on the grey stone Buddha on my windowsill, as he exudes his usual tranquility.

I'm resting my tired heart on your battered breast, darling Earth, as you absorb whatever we hurl at you.

After I rest a while, I might top up the pond for the tadpoles. I might walk through your woods, praising them. I might paint a placard or do my computer busy-work or read about caves or put on a load of washing.

For now, my spirit needs to lie on its back under leaves with the sun soaking through. It needs to float in a cool pool adorned with water-lilies. It needs to curl up under your desk like Ralph the dog, and snore.

Love, Satya

Dear Earth, I'm still not fixed yet, goddammit

I've lived on your lap for forty five years now, darling Earth, and I have done a lot of therapy. I've spent decades in twelve step programmes and trainings, and I've done a lot of spiritual practice. I've consumed forests of books. I've written teetering stacks of journals. And I am *still not fixed*.

There are parts of me that despair when I tip headlong into overwhelm, as I have this week. When I discover new seams of buried shame and aching vulnerability. When I don't 'hold it together', as so many parts of me say I should. They shout from the sidelines. Improve! Streamline! Heal!

I remember your trees, magnificent Earth. I think of ancient apple trees, grown crooked, covered in cankers. Bent walnuts. Ailing ash. As they age, they produce both fresh green growth and brittle old sticks. They don't aim at becoming the 'perfect tree'. They are a mix of processes and, if they're lucky, for a while they'll gift blossom and fruit before crumbling back down into the soil.

This is a gentler way of seeing myself, dear Earth. I am a mix too. Parts of me produce blossoms, and other parts of me are bent, wounded, decaying. I don't like containing vulnerability, but it is there – just as it is in the nature of trees to contain chlorophyll.

Dear Earth, I am a Satya tree. There will be new growth, there will be healing, and there will be calcification and rotting. Some of this is in my control, and much of it is not. I'm looking at myself through your eyes now, sweet

Earth, and maybe I'm not so bad. The sun is out, and the wind is ruffling my leaves.

Love, Satya

Dear Earth, I don't want to look at my racism

I am tired. I am one of the good guys already. I don't want to use the wrong words and be judged. I don't want to take up space. I don't want to crash into any more pockets of shame, anger or despair. I'm afraid of what I'll find inside me.

Darling Earth, we all knelt in silence for eight minutes and forty seconds at the protest today. This is how long it takes to know that a light has been extinguished forever. We felt your steady presence underneath us, and we breathed. There – the grief rises in me again.

Earth, if I want to help heal you, I need to take an unflinching look at myself. I need to see the privileges I enjoy, reliant on the blood and sweat of others. I need to check the assumptions I make. I need to acknowledge how I read 'white' (a sea of faces on Antiques Roadshow, upper management, our own congregation) as 'normal'.

I will get it wrong. I will be called out, and I will try and welcome that, whilst other parts of me resist and try to hide. I will keep finding layers under layers of internalised white supremacy. This ossified fear and hate will be layered with contrition. I will be sorry.

I am sorry, dear Earth, for the racism I contain. I didn't put it all there, and it's my responsibility to root it out.

Love, Satya

Dear Earth, what do you expect from me?

You don't expect the beans outside my window to shoot their winding, dividing tendrils like Jack's beanstalk across the vegetable patch, producing pomegranates, artichokes, bouquets of exotic flowers. You would be happy if they slowly crawl up their bamboo poles and make beautiful runner beans.

You don't expect this little mouse to be peacemaker between our dog and cat, or to learn how to operate a remote controlled car, or to give an impassioned speech to the United Nations about pesticides. You would be happy if she skitters around the vegetable patch, enjoying her bird-seed breakfast, leaving small gifts of compost behind her.

You don't expect whales to learn to jive. It would make you smile if they did, but it isn't necessary.

You don't expect me to save you. You would be happy if today I make bread, fetch hay for the bunnies from the supermarket, see my therapy clients, and write you this love letter.

You know that I'm weary, and you don't need me to burst into action like fireworks today.

You know that I've carried grief for the world this week, and it would make you happy if I sat and watched the silver birch waving in the breeze for a little while.

You never expect more of me than I can manage. It's me that does that. Today I will see the world through your tender gaze, darling Earth, including the mirror.

With much love & gratitude, Satya

Dear Earth, I'm a miracles-do-happen realist

A few weeks ago my Buddhist teacher said that, in relation to what will happen as we come out of lock down, he's a happy pessimist. He believes that, broadly, polluters will spring back to trashing you, shoppers will slide back into unnecessary excess, and those few white men who hold the lion's share of the globe's money will cling onto it just as tightly as before.

If he's a happy pessimist, I've been wondering what I am.

I know that our time is fast running out. I know that human beings are riddled with selfishness. I see it in myself. I know that we are blighted by generations of the injuries we inflict on each another when we are frightened. I carry those wounds. I know that change can require the obliteration of our entire self-constructs. I know how that feels like dying.

I am a realist. And. I have seen miracles happen.

I have seen sixteen year olds arrested for your sake, darling Earth, awake all cold night long in lock-ons. I have seen alcoholics and drug addicts find sobriety, contrition and ordinary joy after decades of dancing with death. I have found contorted, screaming places deep inside me that have transformed into laughing children under the light of love.

We are heading towards extinction. I don't know if it's possible to turn the ship around and, as I've said before, I'll carry on doing the small things I can do either way.

I carry the possibility of miracles with me through these difficult times. Some days, like today, I listen to the soft song of rain and watch the beans spiralling up the bamboo tripods and I know that I'm already inside one.

With tenderness, Satya

Dear Earth, maybe humans really are on their way out

Our government isn't on track to meet their own 2050 carbon targets, which were woefully inadequate to begin with. The Arctic is boiling. The rainforests are being razed. Greed, hate and delusion swirl in us all.

More and more, I'm opening to the possibility that we have entered a terminal phase of our life-span. That it is too late to turn the humanity-ship around.

This morning we walked through the heat in our face masks to deliver a letter to our MP. When someone is dying, you don't stop helping them to come to terms with their reality. You don't stop feeding them blueberries, or giving them medicine for their pain. You don't stop laughing with them.

Will our letters make any difference? I don't know, and it's not my business to know.

It feels good to take action. It's an act of love for you, sweet Earth. We do what small things we can – all of us – and then the results are out of our hands.

If we really are going? I'll be suffering's witness. I'll taste your ripe fruits. I'll leave you with as many offerings as I can.

Love, Satya

Dear Earth, here is wet-dog joy

Our seven dogs hadn't met before. As we swapped polite human pleasantries they sniffed each other's bums and worked out how they might play together. Half-way through our walk, an oasis of water presented itself. They all bounded in, splashing, together, delighted.

Whenever I go online, I encounter thorns. They prick me with news of environmental breakdown and stark political denial. They catch on my clothes when I'm drawn into fierce and polarised arguments. Sometimes they draw blood, or tears.

There are thorns in the real world too. There's no avoiding them. And, the way I use the internet means I end up hurting myself over and over, the thorns all gathered into one place and electrified.

If I am to be of use to you, darling Earth, I need to watch dogs splashing in cool water instead. I need to go away for a week with cake and a teetering pile of books. I need to talk to people who get it. I need to let my eyes feed on the electric blue spray of lobelia, the glossy emerald of chard, the red blobs of runner bean promises.

We need to be wounded to understand wounding. We don't have to seek it out – there is enough happening already. We need to tend to these broken places in ourselves and in others, seek understanding, grow scar tissue, grow compassion. We need to keep our eyes open, dear Earth, and speak up for you.

There is always enough love to salve our wounds, but only if we ask for it. I'm asking. I'm receiving. I'm garnering strength for whatever is next. Today, I'm delighting in the grins of splashing dogs.

Love, Satya

Dear Earth, I surrender

I surrender to not knowing how much longer you will support the human race before shrugging us off.

I surrender to not being your sole heroic saviour.

I surrender to my ordinary life with all its caramel brownies and sore backs, warm bright words from friends and what's-the-point dragging afternoons.

I surrender to the small actions that feel good – organising a prayer vigil for you during the rebellion, caring for the temple garden, responding whenever I can to whatever is here with kindness.

I surrender the results of my actions, and of everyone else's – that's not my business.

I surrender to the beauty of your frilled skirt purple-veined kale, your tree-jewelled hills draped in muslin mist, the roaring yellow of a single dandelion in the lawn.

I surrender to your song, which heals me as it enters me. Right now your leaves are saying shhhhhhhhhhhh.......

Much love, Satya

Dear Earth, I got fatter during lockdown

The kind of fatter than necessitates new trousers.

As usual, this has set off vicious internal arguments. My managing parts resolve to give up sugar as soon as I'm back from holiday. My bingeing parts make me eat three cakes on the journey home whilst I still can. My critical parts yell that I'm weak-willed and pathetic, and that no-one will love me if I don't stop eating. And so on.

Why am I telling you this, darling Earth? Because I think you know about systems that regulate themselves. You are busy absorbing our pollutants, doing what you can to process them.

This is what my system is doing. Living through a pandemic as the world burns is a teensy bit challenging, and my system is trying to steady itself as a result. My sugar-eating parts have been working overtime.

When I see my new fat as a natural consequence of my system trying to steady itself, it doesn't seem so awful. The critical, desperate manager parts of me are just doing their job too. It doesn't mean I'm a bad person. It doesn't mean I'm completely out of control. I can even take a step away from the fat-shaming culture I'm steeped in, and give my tummy rolls an affectionate pat.

Earth, you are doing what you can with the challenges we are throwing at you. My mini-system is doing the same. What can I do to help my bingeing parts? I can notice them, understand them, and appreciate them. I can love them. I can love the parts of me that hate my bingeing parts too.

You always call me to love more of you, darling Earth.

Love Satya

Dear Earth, it's started

It's 5.30am and I've been awake for hours. My brain is fizzing like sherbet. After a crazy-busy week and with a full day ahead of me, I can't find the soft blanket of sleep.

Rebellion is coming. In six weeks we will be out on the streets again – grandfathers, scientists, ex-policemen, pilots, people of faith, new mothers – all of us screaming on your behalf, dear Earth.

Where are these chemicals coming from, lacing my blood with vigilance?

There's grief. The deep ache in my heart when I see what we're doing to you, sweet Earth.

There's fear. The facts we keep hiding from, the terrible times that are coming.

There's anxiety. A surging of the thousands of small tasks that go into planning a rebellion.

There's dread. How will it be to be arrested this time? Who will hate us for what we're doing? How will I hold it all?

More than any of that, there's excitement. Excitement at soon being able to *do* something that I believe will make a difference. A coming together with old comrades and new, a fresh blossoming of the kindest and fiercest society I've known, a place where I learnt that we have way more power than we think we do. That we can change everything.

As a human being I am full of the usual holes. I am not an attentive auntie. I offer this sleeplessness to my young nieces, who marched with me in October. I offer them my hope, as the sun flings light across the valley. I offer them my joy as I imagine their possible golden futures.

As we move through this pandemic, we have an opportunity. We can go back to heating you as quickly as before, dear Earth, or we can stop. We could just stop.

I am awake. I am ready.

With much love, Satya

Postscript

Dear reader, I was arrested twice more during the September rebellion, which took place in London, Cardiff and Manchester. Thousands of people took part in many wonderful and creative actions. There were more than 600 arrests. As I write, the country seems to be preparing for a second lock-down as new cases of coronavirus soar. I am involved in an ongoing vigil for the Earth in my small home town, and many other small scale Extinction Rebellion actions will continue until it is safe to get back on the streets in big numbers. Other groups are also speaking up for the Earth, and for social justice – continuing the good work they've been doing for decades. If you have been inspired by these letters, I'd encourage you to think about effecting system change rather than focusing on individual change. Individual change is important and necessary, but it can distract us from targeting the huge corporations who are causing the vast majority of the climate and ecological devastation. If we continue to work together towards social justice for all, and if we continue to be fuelled by compassion, I believe that we have the power to change everything. Thank you for reading, and I maybe I'll see you on the streets.

Love, Satya

Postscript

Further exploration

If you want to develop your own relationship with the Earth, and think about what you might want to offer her, some suggestions are below.

I offer two free e-courses on my site www.dearearth.co.uk – one to help you learn more about what's happening and think about what you can do, and one on writing 'earthellos'. There is also a 'What Can I Do' section with videos, a book list and other resources. You can read about setting up your own local vigil at www.earthvigil.co.uk.

For me, the thing that made the biggest difference was joining a community of people who were also gravely concerned about the Earth. This group might be Extinction Rebellion, or Greenpeace, or a smaller organisation, or maybe you'll start your own. Keep looking until you find something that fits.

Good luck, and enjoy walking with our beloved Earth.

Lightning Source UK Ltd.
Milton Keynes UK
UKHW011247071021
391819UK00013B/939